CAMBRIDGE LIBRARY COLLECTION

Books of enduring scholarly value

History

The books reissued in this series include accounts of historical events and movements by eye-witnesses and contemporaries, as well as landmark studies that assembled significant source materials or developed new historiographical methods. The series includes work in social, political and military history on a wide range of periods and regions, giving modern scholars ready access to influential publications of the past.

A Review of the Financial Situation of the East India Company in 1824

Henry St George Tucker (1772–1851) sailed to India in 1786 and worked in a number of administrative posts before becoming a director of the East India Company in 1826. He wrote this book following the publication of an essay by French economist Jean-Baptiste Say (1767–1832) which suggested that British possession of territories in India was a burden to the mother country. Tucker's aim with this work was to give an accurate report of the finances of the East India Company in order to show Say's claim to be false. First published in 1825, this book contains an analysis of the company's sources of revenue and gives the details of revenue raised from opium, salt, stamps and land taxes. It includes information on the revenue raised from different territories and finally concludes with an overview of the company's general finances, thus providing valuable data for the study of colonial economics.

Cambridge University Press has long been a pioneer in the reissuing of out-of-print titles from its own backlist, producing digital reprints of books that are still sought after by scholars and students but could not be reprinted economically using traditional technology. The Cambridge Library Collection extends this activity to a wider range of books which are still of importance to researchers and professionals, either for the source material they contain, or as landmarks in the history of their academic discipline.

Drawing from the world-renowned collections in the Cambridge University Library and other partner libraries, and guided by the advice of experts in each subject area, Cambridge University Press is using state-of-the-art scanning machines in its own Printing House to capture the content of each book selected for inclusion. The files are processed to give a consistently clear, crisp image, and the books finished to the high quality standard for which the Press is recognised around the world. The latest print-on-demand technology ensures that the books will remain available indefinitely, and that orders for single or multiple copies can quickly be supplied.

The Cambridge Library Collection brings back to life books of enduring scholarly value (including out-of-copyright works originally issued by other publishers) across a wide range of disciplines in the humanities and social sciences and in science and technology.

A Review of the
Financial Situation
of the
East India Company
in 1824

HENRY ST GEORGE TUCKER

CAMBRIDGE UNIVERSITY PRESS

Cambridge, New York, Melbourne, Madrid, Cape Town,
Singapore, São Paolo, Delhi, Mexico City

Published in the United States of America by Cambridge University Press, New York

www.cambridge.org
Information on this title: www.cambridge.org/9781108046435

© in this compilation Cambridge University Press 2013

This edition first published 1825
This digitally printed version 2013

ISBN 978-1-108-04643-5 Paperback

A

REVIEW,

&c. &c. &c.

A

REVIEW

OF THE

FINANCIAL SITUATION

OF THE

EAST-INDIA COMPANY,

IN 1824.

By HENRY ST. GEORGE TUCKER, ESQ.

LONDON:

PRINTED FOR KINGSBURY, PARBURY, AND ALLEN,

LEADENHALL STREET.

1825.

LONDON:

PRINTED BY COX AND BAYLIS, GREAT QUEEN STREET.

TO

THE RIGHT HONOURABLE

GEORGE CANNING,

&c. &c. &c.

SIR:

As the Friend of India, and as the Minister and Friend of your Country, I presume to address to you the following Essay; not merely for the purpose of paying a just tribute of respect, but with the view of calling your attention to a question, which deeply affects the interests and well-being of the Agricultural Population of British India; and which may, eventually, affect the tranquillity and security of our Possessions in the East.

If I have not mistaken your character, the prospect of doing a public good, or of averting an impending evil, would recom-

mend

mend any question to your best attention; but, associated as you have been in the Administration of India, the People of that Country may be considered to have particular claims upon you ; and I may be permitted to add, that, by exerting your influence to promote the prosperity of this remote, but valuable dependency, you will consult the best interests of the Empire at large, and thus discharge the sacred duty imposed on you as a Minister of the Crown.

I have the honour to be,

With great respect,

SIR,

Your obedient humble servant,

H. ST. G. TUCKER.

Upper Portland Place,
March 1825.

ADVERTISEMENT.

THE following pages were intended to form
part of a larger work ; but, as the undertaking
originally contemplated could not have been
completed for a considerable time ; and as
the subject which these pages embrace is of
more immediate interest ; I have been induced
to submit to the Public the present Essay, de-
tached from other matter. And if I should have
succeeded in exhibiting a distinct Analysis of the
Accounts of the East-India Company, and in
giving a just delineation of the Financial Situation
of that body, I may indulge the hope that I shall
have performed no unacceptable service.

INTRODUCTORY OBSERVATIONS.

ALTHOUGH Great Britain has possessed for more than half a century, in the remote regions of the East, a territory of vast extent, containing a numerous and industrious population, and rich in its manufactures, as well as in the productions of the soil, it still remains a problem whether this possession is to be esteemed a treasure, or the source of weakness to the mother country. That any doubt should exist upon such a question, can arise only from our ignorance of those facts and circumstances upon which the solution of the problem must depend. We are, in truth, very imperfectly acquainted with the state of our empire in the East; our ignorance has produced indifference towards the country and its inhabi-

B   tants;

tants; and it would not be extraordinary if, under the influence of indifference and neglect, a possession, otherwise of the highest value, should become worthless in our hands.

On the continent of Europe the possession of India has hitherto been regarded with very different feelings : for as it has long been observed, that those countries which successively engrossed the commerce of Asia, had all attained an extraordinary degree of wealth, power, and commercial prosperity, it was assumed, and with some appearance of reason, that our territorial dominion in the East had raised Great Britain from her natural level to that high and pre-eminent station which she at present occupies. That the possession of British India has contributed mainly to augment the resources of this country, and to give it weight and influence among the nations of Europe, is a proposition which I have not now to advance for the first time ; but, on the other hand, it is as much a mistake to refer our commercial grandeur, our wealth, and our power, *exclusively* to this source,

as

as it would be to maintain that British India has become a burthen to the mother country.

Strange as it may appear, this latter proposition has now been put forth, and from a quarter where, heretofore, it had been so much the fashion to exaggerate the value of our Eastern possessions. M. Say, one of the most celebrated of the French economists, in an essay lately published, has gravely maintained, that British India is a charge upon this country to the extent of above two millions sterling per annum; and that far from being viewed, as it long has been, by Russia and France with feelings of envy and jealousy, it ought rather to be regarded as an excrescence which wastes and consumes a portion of our vital strength.

If the opinions of this philosopher exercised no influence beyond the continent of Europe, we might safely leave them to produce their effects; and if they tended in any degree to allay the spirit of avarice and the rage of ambition among our continental rivals, we should have reason to congratu-

B 2   late

late them and M. Say on the success of his speculations.

But, unfortunately, there are persons in this country who are sufficiently prone to adopt the same erroneous notions; and whose errors, far from conducing to any salutary end, must exert a baneful influence over the destinies of India.

In all cases, erroneous opinions are liable to produce erroneous measures; and in the present instance, the impression that India is become a bankrupt concern, and a drain upon the resources of the mother country, would not only have a tendency to depreciate the value of the large capital which is invested in the Company's securities, both abroad and at home, but it would also probably lead to a course of policy highly injurious to the interests of both countries.

It is remarkable that, at the very moment when M. Say declares the East-India Company to be in a state of bankruptcy, the Marquess of Hastings should announce to that body the existence of a surplus revenue in India to the amount of four millions sterling

sterling per annum; but these contradictory statements will be found, in both instances, to have been hazarded upon insufficient grounds. A net revenue of four millions has never been realized by the Company, in any one year since our acquisition of territorial dominion in India; nor is it to be desired, I think, that such a revenue should be drawn from the country: but if M. Say's deficit of two millions be deducted from his Lordship's surplus of four millions, a near approximation will be made to the truth.

But the contradictions and errors observable in the different descriptions which have been given of the Company's affairs, and of the condition of British India, are not by any means confined to the financial branch of the subject. The Government has been described as a pure despotism; the ancient institutions of the country are represented to have been wantonly subverted; the rights of the tenantry to have been disregarded and invaded; while the hereditary aristocracy is said to have disappeared

appeared from the face of the land; new systems, unsuitable to the character and habits of the people, and abhorrent to their feelings, are stated to have been introduced by rash innovators; the public revenue is supposed to be extracted from our native subjects by means of grinding monopolies; and, in short, our dominion, far from being recognised as the source of mutual benefit, has been represented as entailing poverty upon India, without producing any corresponding advantage to the mother country.

These sweeping allegations would all require a distinct and particular examination; and he who should faithfully and successfully execute the work, would perform a useful and important service. My present undertaking will be confined within narrower limits, and be directed to an object more within my reach. I propose to offer a digest of the Company's accounts, for the purpose of removing misconceptions upon matters of fact, and of exhibiting a clear and connected view of the present condition of their finances.

It

It is scarcely necessary for me to point out how essential it is, that those who have invested their funds in the securities of the Company, either abroad or at home, should possess correct information with respect to the state of the concern in which their property has been embarked. The public securities of the Indian Governments have been negotiated of late at a premium of near forty per cent., and East-India Stock bears at present a premium of one hundred and ninety per cent.; and it is obviously of the last importance that the creditors abroad, and the proprietors at home, should know whether this enhanced valuation of their capital rests upon any solid foundation. The debt of India is secured on the territory; but this territory M. Say pronounces to be an unproductive possession. The dividends on India Stock are made payable by Act of Parliament from the commercial profits of the Company, and, failing such profits, from the surplus revenue of India; but M. Say declares that there does not exist either profit or surplus. This assertion I shall not find

it

it difficult to controvert; but it will not follow as matter of course that, upon a sober consideration of the Company's situation, financial and political, a rational conclusion can be drawn, either that the present annuity will be guaranteed to the proprietors in perpetuity, or that they will obtain ultimately a full indemnification for the capital which they may have embarked.

Moderate as are my pretensions, I may have engaged in an undertaking beyond my strength: but the question is one which calls for professional experience, rather than for the higher powers of mind; and as I shall not deviate far from the beaten path which has long been familiar to me, the reader will not, I hope, see occasion to charge me with presumption.

A

R E V I E W,

&c. &c.

CHAPTER I.

TERRITORIAL REVENUE OF BRITISH INDIA.

" On est donc fondé à regarder la Compagnie Anglaise des Indes comme
" une association, tout à la fois commerçante et souveraine, qui, ne gagnant
" rien ni dans sa souveraineté, ni dans son commerce, est réduite à emprunter
" chaque année de quoi distribuer à ses actionnaires un semblant de profit."
—*Essai Historique, etc. Par J. B. Say.*

M. Say, in a late essay published in " la Revue Encyclopédique," has exhibited a statement
of the finances of the East-India Company, which
is not only unsupported by any recent documents,
but which is completely at variance with the
public accounts annually submitted to the British
Parliament under the sanction of the highest authority.

This writer has too high a reputation at stake to
put forth a statement intended to mislead ; and

the

the just and liberal admissions which he seems
disposed to make in favour of our administration of
India, furnish a presumption that he is by no means
deficient in that spirit of candour, which should
characterize the philosopher and the historian.
M. Say would appear, however, to have consulted very old authorities, and to have taken as
the foundation of his estimates the results of a
year of actual war, or averages deduced from a
series of years, in which war very generally pre-
vailed. But if this be the correct mode of proceeding for the purpose of ascertaining the financial situation of a country, in what kingdom of
Europe shall we discover any thing beyond the
traces of a deplorable bankruptcy? If an average
of thirty years were taken for the purpose of de-
termining the revenue and charge of Great Britain,
instead of an annual surplus of five millions applicable to the extinction of debt, should we not
be appalled with the re-appearance of a spectre
which once threatened to paralize the energies of
this nation? If the process apparently adopted by
M. Say were applied to this country, we should
be found struggling still with an annual deficit
of twenty millions, instead of scattering, with a
lavish hand, our surplus capital over every part of
the civilized world.

In India we have had our full share of warfare
in common with the rest of mankind, and we
have

have not only been engaged in wars, originating in our own local and peculiar objects and interests, but we have incidentally been led into hostilities, whose origin could be distinctly traced to the political relations of the parent state in Europe. The late Sultan of Mysore, after having been subdued and stript of half his dominions, would scarcely have dared, single-handed, to provoke that power which had overthrown him in the fulness of his strength, if he had not been encouraged to expect a powerful auxiliary in the republican government of France. The fabulous representations and extravagant suggestions of an obscure French adventurer,* stimulating the pride, the restless ambition, and deep-rooted resentment of Tippoo Sultan, engaged him to make overtures to the Governor of the Isle of France, which not only manifested a hostile

---

* This is an instance of the most important events being produced by very mean instruments. *Ripaud*, the French adventurer alluded to, had been the master of a small privateer, and was detained by Tippoo Sultan at Seringapatam. To extricate himself from this state of durance which had become extremely irksome to him, he represented to the Sultan that there were fleets and armies at the Isle of France ready to obey his call, and that he had only to despatch him (*Ripaud*) to the Island in order to obtain a force, which would enable him to crush his mortal enemy, the English. The papers of this Frenchman, which were found at Seringapatam after the capture of that place, are extremely curious.

a hostile spirit, but which justified the Marquess
of Wellesley in proceeding against that infatuated
despot as the ally of France and the enemy of the
British power.

In the same manner the ascendancy of a French
party at Hyderabad gave occasion to that bold
and masterly enterprize of Lord Wellesley's Government, by which a large army, disciplined
and commanded by French officers, was suddenly
surrounded and disarmed without the loss of a
man. So, also, the predominance of French influence at the Court of Dowlut Rao Scindiah,
and the formidable position occupied by the numerous forces of General Perron on our most
accessible frontier, furnished perhaps the best
justification of those extensive military operations
which, in 1804, terminated in the expulsion of
the Mahratta power from the North of Hindoostan, and in placing the imperial city of Delhi
and the once august house of Timour, under the
protection of a company of British merchants.

The wars in which the Marquess of Hastings
engaged had their origin, it is true, in our local
politics, and may be regarded as exclusively our
own. We had no French interests to counteract
or destroy : no French Generals to displace or
overthrow ; and if these wars were of annual oc-
currence, or of continued duration, the statement
of M. Say, with respect to the pecuniary value
of

of our Indian possessions, would not be entirely destitute of foundation.

Without, however, indulging in speculations, either with regard to the past or the future, I will proceed to exhibit the actual result of the account of Indian revenue and expenditure for a period of thirty years; and as this statement has been prepared from official and authentic documents, it may be received with confidence.

GOVERNMENT.	Surplus in Sicca Rupees.	Deficit in Sicca Rupees.
1792-3* Lord Cornwallis' 1,65,57,675		
1793-4* Lord Cornwallis' and		
Lord Teignmouth's..1,22,12,636		
1794-5..Lord Teignmouth's .. 94,58,486		
1795-6.. Do.............. .. 64,66,225		
1796-7.. Do............. .. 19,70,197		
1797-8.. Do.......................		32,73,982
1798-9..Lord Wellesley's..............		75,97,009
1799-1800 Do.........................		14,10,455
1800-1.. Do.........................		89,16,178
1801-2.. Do.........................		4,01,211
1802-3.. Do.............. 96,35,832		
1803-4.. Do.........................		98,95,346
1804-5.. Do.........................		2,69,69,509

* In the revenue of 1792-3 is included the sum of Sicca Rupees 16,83,514; and in that of 1793-4, the sum of Sicca Rupees 33,67,028, received at Fort St. George from the late Tippoo Sultan in satisfaction of the conditions of the treaty concluded with Lord Cornwallis. So, also, in 1815-16, the sum of Sicca Rupees 95,68,750 was received from the Nawaub of Oude for the cession of Kyraghur; and although none of these sums properly constitute *revenue*, they augment the surplus.

GOVERNMENT.	Surplus in Sicca Rupees.	Deficit in Sicca Rupees.
1805-6* Lord W.'s and Sir G. Barlow's		2,86,49,795
1806-7..Sir G. Barlow's and Lord Minto's		1,02,06,904
1807-8 ..Lord Minto's	10,39,730	
1808-9 .. Do.	5,25,883	
1809-10.. Do.	33,16,866	
1810-11.. Do.	42,36,094	
1811-12.. Do.	1,30,47,521	
1812-13.. Do.	83,04,269	
1813-14..Lord Minto's and Lord Hastings'	1,45,33,190	
1814-15..Lord Hastings' ...	1,18,57,412	
1815-16.. Do.............	35,77,488	
1816 17.. Do.............	1,09,37,338	
1817-18.. Do.............	41,70,103	
1818-19.. Do.		11,77,201
1819-20.. Do.		16,51,241
1820-21.. Do.............	1,09,68,799	
1821-22†.. Do.............	1,76,33,616	

If
surplus. They may be regarded as a receipt for defraying the extra-ordinary war charge.

* Lord Cornwallis, on his return to India, held the Government only for about three months.

† Statements of this kind are usually thrown into an Appendix; but this is sometimes to throw them out of sight, and I am desirous that the alternations of our Indian revenue, should appear in one connected view in this place as a basis for my subsequent remarks. The annual surplus is exhibited in the Calcutta sicca rupee; for as that currency is reduced into English money by different parties at different rates of exchange, no accurate comparison could be drawn between the revenue of particular years, unless one common standard were assumed for the whole.

If the revenues of India were not liable to any deductions, the foregoing statement would furnish a most satisfactory picture of the financial re· sources of British India, since, notwithstanding the many expensive wars in which we have been engaged, we should appear to have realized within the thirty years a considerable surplus beyond the local expenditure (including the interest of the public debt), after deducting the deficit which occurred in particular years of the term. In fact, there is this distinction between the wars carried on by the States of Europe and those in which our Indian Government have engaged, that while the one, after inflicting mutual injuries and incurring an enormous expenditure of money, generally terminate in the *status quo ante,* the other have usually been attended with an accession of territory and revenue, and sometimes with pecuniary indemnification for the expenses incurred in maintaining our political ascendancy.

But the surplus revenue realized in India cannot all be considered as clear and independent income, subject to no further deduction, for there is a large disbursement in this country on account of our Eastern possessions, which is not included in the Indian accounts, but which properly constitutes a charge upon the local revenue. This disbursement was heretofore inconsiderable ; but from the augmentation of our army and other

causes,

causes, it has gradually increased, and it now amounts to a large sum annually. No useful purpose would be answered by exhibiting the particulars of the home charge for a series of years, nor indeed are there materials for a retrospect beyond the year 1813,* when the political and commercial charges were, for the first time, separated and particularly distinguished ; and I shall therefore confine myself in this place to a statement of the disbursements in the two last years, which will sufficiently shew their nature and extent.

Statement of territorial, or political charges, incurred in England on account of India :

1821-22.

Military and Marine Stores supplied from England	£306,489
Payments on account of furlough and allowances to retired officers	257,808
Passage-money to officers and troops	69,447
Political Freight, &c.	142,944
Interest and Charges on account of the Carnatic Debt	85,123
Disbursements on account of St. Helena	150,962
Do. on account of Bencoolen	479
Do. on account of Prince of Wales' Island	2,426
Political Charges General (Establishments at the India-House, &c. &c.)	371,070
Total	£1,386,748

* Prior to 1812-13, the home charge appears to have been *estimated* by the Court of Directors at £850,000 per annum.

1822-23.

1822-23.

Military and Marine Stores	£348,426
Furlough and retired officers	261,071
Passage money	102,092
Political freight	106,452
Carnatic debt	96,013
St. Helena	117,498
Bencoolen and Prince of Wales' Island	11,110
Political charges general	391,665
Total..	£1,434,327

It is not my intention to enter into an examination of these charges. Some of them may
possibly be reduced hereafter; but in general,
they may be considered in a course of increase;
for in consequence of the recent augmentation of
the Indian army, a greater number of officers
may be expected to come upon the retired list,
while the late regulations for dividing the regi-
ments and otherwise accelerating promotion, will
place upon that list, at an earlier period, officers
entitled by their rank to higher allowances.
Far, indeed, am I from intimating the slightest
objection to these just and salutary concessions
to our Indian army: my business is to explain
their effects. There is, indeed, an elastic force
in expenditure, which makes it difficult for
the most prudent government to repress it;
and in the instance under consideration, we must
be prepared for a further increase of charge.

D The

The territorial disbursement in England already amounts to a million and a half sterling * per annum ; and it cannot safely be estimated below that standard in any prospective calculation which may be made to determine the surplus revenue of India.

The following abstract will shew the net surplus drawn from British India in 1821-22, and the expected surplus of 1822-23, respectively.

Surplus revenue realized in India in 1821-22,   **£.**
deducting St. Helena .... †1,927,263
Deduct:
Amount of territorial charge disbursed in
England in 1821-22, exclusive of St. Helena 1,235,786

      Net surplus revenue in 1821-22 ..   £691,477
                                    Indian

* I have seen this charge variously stated; but I have satisfied myself completely that it amounts at present to £1,500,000 *at the least*. It is, indeed, estimated this year at £1,535,288.

† The surplus of 1821-22 was stated above in Sicca Rupees at 1,76,33,616. The intrinsic or bullion value of the Sicca Rupee is 2s. 566d., and this is also nearly its present value in exchange, although the exchange has fluctuated between wide extremes, *i.e.* from 2s. 10d. down to 1s. 10d. the Sicca Rupee. In exhibiting the surplus in English money, I have followed the printed statements in which the *current* rupee is valued at two shillings. This rate exceeds both its bullion value and its present value in exchange. Lord Hastings has stated the sicca rupee at 2s. 6d. which makes the revenue appear higher. It is proper to point out that discrepances occasionally occur in the printed statements which I have not always the means of reconciling. For example: in the account printed under date the 8th July 1823, the Indian surplus of 1821-22 is stated at £2,111,337, or deducting St. Helena at £1,995,033; whereas, in the account published under
                                     date

Indian surplus of 1822-23 per estimate *2,274,646
Deduct :
Territorial charge in England in 1822 23,
   exclusive of St. Helena 1,316,829

Estimated net surplus in 1822-23... £957,817

It will be apparent from this abstract that M. Say, in estimating an annual deficit of fifty-seven † millions of francs, or £2,280,000 upon our Indian account of revenue and charge, is completely in error ; while the Marquess of Hastings, from a very natural feeling, has taken too favourable a view of our financial situation and prospects.

M. Say has perhaps considered that a corroboration of his assumption of a deficit will be found in the rapid increase of the public debt of India ; but it is very possible for the *local* debt to increase, even during the existence of a territorial *surplus,* since that surplus may be transferred

to

date the 13th May 1824, the surplus of the same year is stated at £1,927,263. I have followed the latest account as likely to be the most accurate. The difference seems to have arisen chiefly on the adjustment of the St. Helena account, the charge for this island being stated in one account at £116,304, and in the other at £208,038.

* I have the satisfaction to learn from private sources, that this estimate has been exceeded in the sum of about £300,000, making the surplus about £2,600,000.

† M. Say, taking the accounts of 1806 as his basis, estimates the territorial deficit at 57 millions, and the commercial loss at 11 millions—together 68 millions francs.

to England or to China, for the purpose of discharging debt, or for other services, or it may become an addition to the *local assets* (the cash balances, &c.) which constitute a fund applicable to the liquidation of debt. It will be useful, however, to trace the progress of the Indian debt, and with this view I have prepared two statements A and B, which will be found in the appendix. The one is formed from the Indian accounts and correspondence, as far as they were accessible to me, and exhibits the debt in *Sicca Rupees* from the year 1793 : the other has been prepared from the accounts which are printed in this country for the use of Parliament, and exhibits both the *debt* and *assets, in English money,* at the end of each year, from 1814. Referring to these accounts for more detailed information, it appears to me essential only to state in this place the amount of the debt at particular periods, and I have selected the years 1793, 1798, 1805, 1814, and 1821, for the purpose of shewing its periodical increase.

Public debt of India *bearing interest :*

	Principal.	Annual Interest.
On the 30th April 1793, Sa. Rs.	5,33,68,683	45,58,798
Do. 1798,	7,57,04,769	48,96,510
Do. 1805,	19,09,71,445	1,39,98,771
Do. 1814,	21,39,92,502	1,27,93,896
Do. 1821,	27,92,31,000	1,70 68,261

In

In order that I may be enabled at the same time to bring M. Say's statement of the Indian debt to a decisive test, it will be necessary for me to enter into a little detail. M. Say has not specified the precise period to which his general remarks apply ; nor the documents from which some of his inferences are drawn ; but in stating the Indian debt at *640 millions of francs, or £25,600,000, he has expressly referred to the accounts of 1805.

The debt of India in that year was Sicca Rupees 19,09,71,445, as stated above, and valuing the rupee at 2s. 6d., the rate probably assumed by M. Say, that writer's statement in the first instance is not materially overcharged ; but he afterwards falls into a most unaccountable mistake, and contrives to augment the Company's imcumbrances in the aggregate, including the home

* " D'après cet exposé; on sera peu surpris que la Compagnie des Indes soit si prodigieusement endette, soit aux Indes, soit en Europe, d'autant mieux que, malgré ses pertes, elle n'a jamais cessé de payer à ses actionnaires un dividende de 10¼ pour cent. En 1805 elle avouait une dette en Angleterre de 150 millions et dans l'Inde de 640, en tout 790 millions. Mais j'observe qu'elle n'établit cette dette, qu'après en avoir déduit les répétitions qu'elle se croit en droit de former. Or, si ces répétitions ne sont pour la plupart composées que de mauvaises créances, dont il est impossible qu'elle soit jamais payée, elles ne sauraient passer pour un actif qu'on puisse employer à diminuer les dettes passives."—P. 289. M. Say appears to have drawn some of his materials from the " History of British India," vol. 3.; but if his statements had been perfectly correct, our *present* situation is surely not to be deduced by going back to the year 1805.

home debt of 150 millions of francs, (or six millions sterling,) to the enormous sum of 1,200 millions of francs, or £48,000,000.*

He first alleges that the sum of £25,600,000 is the amount of our Indian debt, *after deducting the amount of assets*, and that in these assets we have included what is technically termed "dead stock," or the value of forst, buildings, furniture, bad debts, and the like; and he, therefore, proceeds to add the sum of 400 millions francs, or sixteen millions sterling, to our acknowledged debt, for the purpose of exhibiting, as he conceives, the real condition of our finances.

But it is not true that in arriving at the sum quoted by M. Say, the "dead stock," or even the "quick stock," had been deducted from the Indian debt, although the latter, consisting as it does of cash and other available assets, must be deducted in order to shew the true state of the Company's affairs; and that writer has consequently committed a two-fold mistake, first, in assuming a deduction to have been made which never was made; and next, in *adding* to the assumed debt of £25,600,000, a sum whih , if correct, ought to have been *deducted* from it.

But

* " Or, toutes ces mauvaises créances ne s'élevant pas à moins de 400 millions, lesquels ne devant pas être déduits, ainsi que le prétend la Compagnie, de sa dette avouée de 790 millions, laissent le principal de cette dette de près de 1,200 millions de notre monnaie."—P. 290.

But without going so far back as the year 1805, for the purpose of ascertaining our *present* condition, I will subjoin an account of the Indian debt and credits on the 30th April 1822, extracted from the printed statements which were laid before parliament in the last sessions, and which are the latest documents at present before the public.

	£.
Amount of bond, register, and other debts bearing interest	31,623,780
Arrears and debts not bearing interest	6,966,877

Gross amount of territorial debt on the 30th April 1822	*38,590,657

Deduct, territorial assets :	£.
Cash in the public treasuries . .	10,634,459
Bills receivable	449,475
Stores	3,027,818
Debts owing to Government	6,412,023
Salt, opium, grain, &c. in store	1,680,929

Total amount of territorial assets	22,204,704

Net excess of territorial debts in India beyond the assets	£16,385,953

It will be seen, then, that instead of an overwhelming debt in India of forty-eight millions sterling,

* The Indian coins are converted into English money at the Company's established rates, to which I have generally adhered, in order that my statement may be more easily verified by a reference to the document from which it is taken.

sterling, with which M. Say has alarmed our imaginations, the actual incumbrance amounts only to £16,385,953, or less than a year's revenue, without taking credit for those fortifications and other immovable property, which, as he justly observes, do not constitute disposable possessions, and which must be left to our successors, whenever we may happen to be deprived of the sovereignty.

Nor have I taken credit for the commercial assets in India, amounting to about £3,000,000, being unwilling to confound the commercial with the territorial account; but had the two been embodied together, the local debt would have been reduced to the sum of £13,404,998.

It may be apprehended that a portion of the political assets, (such as the value of stores, debts owing to the government, &c.) cannot justly be regarded as a real available resource, applicable to the discharge of debt.

It is certainly true that we cannot tender to our creditors military and marine stores in satisfaction of their legal claims upon us; but it is equally true that these indispensable articles have been procured at a certain cost; that they represent a certain determinate value; and that this value is ultimately realized, since, on being used or expended, they serve to defray charge, and

prevent

prevent the disbursement which must otherwise have taken place in procuring them.

The amount of what is termed "dead stock" is not calculated upon by the Company to any extent as a set-off* against their debt, although this property, in which M. Say considers them to possess only an usufructuary interest, is kept in sight with a view to some future adjustment with the crown. The "quick stock," on the contrary, should contain only genuine funds, capable of being realized; and as far as my experience extends, the public officers are sufficiently careful to exclude from that account all items of a questionable character, whose introduction might tend to mislead.

In order to prevent the attention from being embarrassed by the accumulation of figures, I have stated merely the *surplus*, or *deficit*, of India in each of the last thirty years, without exhibiting the account of revenue and charge from which the results are deduced; but as our information would be incomplete if this account were omitted altogether, I shall subjoin an abstract of it for five years, selecting those periods which appear to me best calculated to shew the progress of our Indian revenue.

LORD

* Credit has been taken in some of the Company's statements for "Dead Stock," to the amount of £400,000 out of above ten millions.

E

1792-3—LORD CORNWALLIS' ADMINISTRTION.

	Revenue.		Charge.		Surplus.	Deficit.
Bengal ...Ct. Rups.	5,52,69,339	£5,526,934	3,21,34,108	£3,213,411	£*2,313,523	—
Madras ....Pags.	61,90,775	2,476,310	53,50,767	2,140,307	336,003	—
Bombay......Rups.	21,02,707	236,555	65,68,899	739,000	—	502,445

1797-8—LORD TEIGNMOUTH'S ADMINISTRATION.

	Revenue.		Charge.		Surplus.	Deficit.
Bengal ...Ct. Rups.	6,15,36,152	6,153,615	3,90,19,775	3,901,977	*2,251,638	—
Madras ....Pags.	48,47,377	1,938,950	62,94,436	2,517,774	—	578,824
Bombay ......Rups.	30,06,129	338,189	84,48,997	950,512	—	612,323

1804-5—LORD WELLESLEY'S ADMINISTRATION.

	Revenue.		Charge.		Surplus.	Deficit.
Bengal. ...Ct. Rups.	9,33,67,070	9,336,707	6,50,82,003	6,508,200	*2,828,507	—
Madras . ...Pags.	1,22,42,852	4,897,140	1,49,79,371	5,991,748	—	1,094,608
Bombay ......Rups.	63,60,436	715,548	1,82,08,775	2,048,487	—	1,332,939

1813-14—LORD MINTO'S ADMINISTRATION.

	Revenue.		Charge.		Surplus.	Deficit.
Bengal ...Ct. Rups.	11,14,11,288	11,141,128	7,10,38,299	7,103,829	*4,037,299	—
Madras ....Pags.	1,31,79,304	5,271,722	1,23,25,813	4,930,325	341,397	—
Bombay......Rups.	64,20,569	722,313	1,36,41,834	1,534,706	—	812,393

1821-22—LORD HASTINGS' ADMINISTRATION.

	Revenue.		Charge.		Surplus.	Deficit.
Bengal .... Ct. Rups.	13,34,05,024	13,340,502	8,54,01,821	8,540,182	*4,800,320	—
Madras .... Pags.	1,38,92,573	5,557,129	1,35,13,980	5,405,592	151,537	—
Bombay...... Rups.	2,53,84,363	2,855,741	3,20,87,955	3,609,894	—	754,153

* This is the *gross* surplus, and not the *net* surplus, after deducting the charge of interest. The statement is intended to shew the gross annual revenue and charge.

The great increase of the revenue will naturally attract attention ; but the amount of the gross revenue of a country does not afford a correct standard for judging of the condition of its finances. If we were to apply this scale of measurement, Great Britain would appear to have reached the utmost height of her prosperity during the most calamitous periods of the late war, for her income was then at the highest ; and she might be considered to have since declined, and to be verging now towards a state of poverty and decay, because her taxes are less productive than heretofore. So, too, in India, it would be fallacious to draw any conclusions from the amount of the *gross* revenue. The increase of income has, in general, arisen from the acquisition of new territory ; but the new territory has brought with it, its own peculiar charge, which in general has equalled, or nearly equalled, the new resource. The Marquess of Hastings has observed, " I have no hesitation in saying that " the increase of the current year 1822-23, may " be anticipated as exceeding by six millions " sterling that of 1813-14 ;" but his Lordship seems to have been aware that the increase of charge, in a certain degree, kept pace with the increase of resource, for he soon after adds, " After revolving every circumstance with the " coolest caution, I cannot find any reason why,

E 2   " subse-

" subsequently to the present year, an annual
" surplus of four millions sterling should not be
" confidently reckoned upon. This ought natu-
" rally to increase, for the causes which will
" augment the receipt have nothing in them tend-
" ing to require further charges."

I have the utmost deference for such high
authority ; but following, as I have done, the
statements printed for the use of parliament, I
have already stated the Indian surplus of 1821-22
at £1,927,263, (or, if St. Helena be omitted,
£2,135,301,) and the surplus estimated for the
year 1882-23 at *£2,274,646, (or, omitting St.
Helena, £2,394,739.) What the revenue may
be hereafter it is impossible for me to predict ; but
I shall submit in the sequel certain considerations
which dispose me to believe that we have less
reason to anticipate an increase than we have to
apprehend a diminution of the territorial income
in future years.

If I were called upon to point out the period
when the Company's finances abroad were in the
most prosperous state, I should probably fix on
the year 1792-93, for we then possessed an annual
surplus sufficient to liquidate the territorial debt

in

* I have great satisfaction in stating, from private information recently received, that the surplus of 1822-23 amounted to about
£2,600,000, the largest revenue ever realized from British India.

in little more than three years.* The territorial
charge incurred in England was inconsiderable ;
our possessions were more compact and manage-
able, and more productive with reference to their
extent ; and the produce and manufactures of India being in great demand in the west, our remittances could be effected on advantageous terms in
commodities, produced by the labour of an industrious population. But it did not certainly depend
upon us to give permanency to our commercial
advantages ; nor was it, perhaps, in our option
to continue in the same political situation : having
once crossed the Caramnassa, our progress successively to the Jumna and Sutlege was, perhaps,
inevitable. We were drawn on by a sort of gra-
vitation, to fill that vacuum ; to occupy that
waste which the desolating policy of the native
states had produced, until we found ourselves in
the possession of a sovereignty, without a parallel
in the history of the world.

But although the Company were in a condition
of greater affluence about the close of Lord Cornwallis's administration than at any other period,
much remained to be done in the way of financial
arrangement ; the rates of interest were high, and
fluctuated

	Debt.	Surplus.		Purchase. Yrs. Mths.	
* 1792-3	5,33,68,683	1,65,57,675	equal to about	3	3
1813-14	21,39,92,502	1,45,33,190		14	9
1821-22	27,27,86,000	1,76,32,616		15	5

fluctuated suddenly and between wide extremes; the theory of exchanges was little understood, or seldom acted upon; the gold and silver coins, which circulated indifferently, did not bear a determinate value with relation to each other, and the latter could not sometimes be procured, even by the government itself, without a sacrifice of 5 or 6 per cent.; a capital had not accumulated commensurate with the agricultural and commercial wants and resources of the country; the natives had not learnt to place confidence in our public securities or to bring the limited funds which they possessed into active and useful employment; and, in short, what is termed " *Public Credit*" had scarcely been called into existence.

During the greater part of Lord Wellesley's administration we were engaged in expensive wars, and the utmost difficulty was experienced in providing for the public expenditure. This consequently was not a favourable season for introducing financial improvements; but the comprehensive mind of that nobleman fully appreciated the value of a well-regulated system of finance; and by the establishment of a public bank and other salutary arrangements, a foundation was laid for those important operations which his successors prosecuted with such eminent success; the tree was planted in this administration; it grew under the fostering care of Sir G. Barlow

and

31

and the Earl of Minto ; and the Marquess of
Hastings had the merit (and it was no inconsiderable merit) of diligently gathering, and carefully
preserving the fruit : hence the noble Marquess
was enabled to carry on extensive military operations throughout the whole frontier of Nepaul;
in Hindoostan and the Deccan, without experiencing those* pecuniary difficulties which had so
much embarrassed his predecessors. It will not
be contended that financial resources can be gene-
rated in a moment to meet the emergency of particular occasions; they are the growth of time;
public credit cannot, like a hot-house plant, be
forced out of season into existence ; it is the off-
spring of confidence ; and confidence is the result
of experience.

It is very far from my wish to under-rate the
merits of Lord Hastings' administration ; but
justice

* We obtained, it is true, about 2,00,00,000 rupees (or about two
millions sterling) from the King of Oude, and the sum of 53,00,000
Sicca Rupees (more than half a million) from the estate of the Bhow
Begum; and these large supplies enabled Lord Hastings to carry on
his wars without experiencing those pecuniary difficulties which
Lord Wellesley had to contend with.

1st. Loan from the King of Oude as a fund for the
payment of annuities to his family .... Sicca Rupees 1,03,82,093
2d. Loan, which was afterwards satisfied by ceding
to his Majesty the districts of Kyraghur, conquered from
the Rajah of Nepaul 95,68,750
Treasure of the late Bhow Begum, committed to our
custody 53,00,000

justice is due to the memory of his predecessor ; and where genuine merit exists, it cannot be tarnished or diminished, by the proximity of merit.

We owe much to the prudent and judicious management of Lord Minto ; the previous wars in which we had been involved had left us in a state of complete* exhaustion ; but the pacific policy which his Lordship pursued, gave us time to recruit and improve our resources, and enabled the Government of India to adopt a course of measures, military and political, of the utmost importance to the public welfare.

I shall only notice two circumstances which more particularly distinguish his Lordship's administration of the finances ; the one, the reduction of the rate of interest on the Indian debt from 8 to 6 per cent., by which a saving of charge to the extent of about half a million sterling per annum, was effected in perpetuity ; the other, the remittance of a large supply of bullion to this country, at a time when the precious metals had nearly disappeared from every part of the empire, and

* It is not my plan to enter into details further than may be necessary to trace and explain our present situation. Otherwise it would be easy for me to set forth the pecuniary difficulties and distress produced by the Mahratta wars of 1803 and 1804, and to shew what extraordinary exertions were required to surmount those difficulties.

and when they were urgently required to enable Great Britain to prosecute to a successful issue the most fearful struggle in which she had ever been engaged.

But, in the letter addressed to the Court of Directors by the Marquess of Hastings, it is intimated that his Lordship took charge of the Government at a season of pecuniary distress; and this statement is corroborated by the tenor of the correspondence from India (recently published by the Court of Directors), at the period in question.

The temporary distress alluded to is, however, easily explained. It was, in part, that of the commercial community. In a country where the rate of interest is high, the merchant has a strong motive for economizing his funds as much as possible; and, when unexpected demands occur, he is liable to be exposed to temporary inconvenience and distress : such precisely was the case in India about the period of his Lordship's arrival. An emergency had arisen among the commercial community of Calcutta ; but the Government very properly came forward to their relief; and, by granting temporary loans to those who required assistance, the cloud passed over without producing any serious mischief.

The government treasury was, also, I am aware, reduced to a low ebb at the period

F   in

in question : but this proceeded entirely from our overstrained* efforts to effect large remittances to England. The living spring was drained for the moment ; but it was not destroyed. Embarrassed as we were, in some degree, at the instant, the government consigned to the Court of Directors, in the *very ship which conveyed Lord Hastings to India,* the sum of three hundred thousand. pounds in specie and bullion ; nor could it have been prepared in 1815 to undertake an expensive war, if at the close of 1813, the sources of our prosperity had not remained unimpaired and abundant.

The Marquess of Hastings unquestionably left the finances of India in a most flourishing condition. Hostilities had been carried on upon an extensive scale without causing any very large addition

---

* Excess of supply to London, 1811-12......Sa. Rups. 3,46,49,832
        Ditto 1812-13 2,71,49,075
Estimated Ditto 1813-14 1,80,00,000

                           Sa. Rups. 7,97,98,907

Or, at 2s. 6d. per Sa. Rups........................... £4,331,229
        Ditto 3,393,634
        Ditto 2,000,000

                                 £9,724,868

(See Financial Despatch from Bengal, dated 18th December 1813.)

dition to be made to the public burthens.* The public treasuries contained the enormous sum of *ten millions sterling ;* the territorial surplus might fairly be assumed at two millions sterling per annum ; a disposable fund of from three to four millions sterling was ready to be applied to the extinction of debt; the government remittable securities, bearing an interest of six per cent., had risen to a premium of near forty per cent., and " public credit" shewed every symptom of health and maturity. This is a splendid picture of financial prosperity ; but its merits are scarcely enhanced by comparison. It will be found, I think, that we possessed in 1813-14 all the elements of financial prosperity in as sound a condition

* The sum of Rupees 95,68,750, received from the King of Oude, for the sale of Kyraghur, reduced the military charge of 1815-16. Large consignments in bullion were also received from England, remitted from the " Surplus Fund of Commercial Profit ;" and these tended materially to prevent the increase of debt, and to facilitate all the financial operations of the Government abroad. Still, it is but just to Lord Hastings, to notice, that his Lordship's military expenditure, as compared with that in the preceding Mahratta war, was very moderate, as was shewn by the Commissary-General. This is to be ascribed, partly to the establishment of an efficient Commissariat by Sir George Hewett, during the administration of Lord Minto, partly to the extent of our pecuniary resources, which enabled the Government to discharge the irregular troops the moment their services were no longer wanted, and partly to the strict attention paid by Lord Hastings to economy in his military dispositions as Commander-in-chief.

dition as in 1822-23. Our territorial debt and the annual charge of interest were less; our surplus revenue was nearly the same; and although we did not possess the same amount of specie, it must not be forgotten that the present accumulation of funds in India originates in circumstances which constitute a *positive evil*. The decrease in the exports from India, consequent to a very extraordinary revolution in the course of the trade, created the utmost difficulty in effecting remittances from that country to England; and individuals were compelled to purchase, at a high premium, the bills which the government were under engagement to grant to the public creditors in payment of the interest on the territorial debt. The payment being thus transferred from the Indian to the home treasury, the former was relieved from an annual demand to the amount of above a million and a half sterling, and a corresponding accumulation of funds took place in the Indian treasuries in consequence. A portion, therefore, of the ten millions of specie with which the local treasuries are surcharged, must not be viewed as *capital saved from a surplus revenue*. It is capital which has remained in *India* from the want of means to remove it to *London*; and both the cause and the effect are to be regarded as matter of regret rather than of gratulation.

The

The fall in the exchange suggested to Lord Hastings, as well as to the Court of Directors, the practicability and expediency of effecting a reduction in the rate of exchange, at which the public creditors were entitled to a remittance for the interest of the territorial debt, and a course of measures was accordingly commenced by his Lordship for this purpose early in 1821, with the concurrence of the Honourable Court. The operation succeeded completely ; the rate of exchange was reduced from $2s. 6d.$ to $2s. 1d.$ the sicca rupee ; and as long as the present exchanges continue, a saving to the Company will probably be effected to the extent of twenty per cent. on the annual interest, for which they were under engagement to furnish a remittance.

I have already presumed to submit my opinion on this subject to the public : and I should not now recur to it, if the measure did not form a distinguishing feature in Lord Hastings' administration of the finances ; and if, in passing it over unnoticed, I might not be supposed to keep out of view a plan of singular merit.

If the object proposed was valuable and desirable in itself, it has been accomplished in the completest manner ; if no future evil should result, the Company have been relieved from an apprehended inconvenience, and an immediate expense : nor will I urge as an objection, that
they

they have smoothed the way for the crown to undertake the management of the territory. The obligation to pay the interest of the debt in England, opposed one great obstacle to the resumption of the charter; because it was heretofore maintained that the Company constituted the only safe and convenient organ of remittance. That obligation has now been withdrawn in a great degree; the Company have succeeded in rendering a large portion of the territorial debt *a local demand*, the interest of which is payable only in India; and as the local revenue is quite adequate to the payment, the crown, in assuming the territory, would have no inconvenient engagements or financial difficulties to encounter. In affording facilities to our successors, there may be nothing exceptionable, if the measure be right in itself, for the end and aim of every public measure ought to be the public good, without regard to partial and temporary interests. My object, indeed, in recurring to past transactions, has not been to discover defects. The great use of a retrospect to the past is to obtain a proper guide for the future. But if it be true that the sudden and extreme depression of the exchange, although originating in causes beyond our controul, were an evil, as I conceive it to have been, then would I submit that, instead of aggravating it by availing ourselves to the utmost of a temporary advantage, our object should have been, and should still be, to alleviate its effects by all unobjectionable means.

From the statement given in a preceding page of the result of the accounts for the last thirty years, it will have appeared that, in nineteen years of the term, a surplus has been realized in India; and when it is recollected that the intervals of peace during this period were short and interrupted, and that the wars carried on embraced objects of no ordinary magnitude, it is as much matter of surprise as of satisfaction, that the event should have been so favourable.

In the calm and prudent administration of Lord Teignmouth, we had a Rohilla war; a revolution in Oude; a formidable demonstration of defensive war against the Affghan state of Caubul; and, lastly, an expedition against the Phillippine Islands, which was arrested in mid-career at Penang.

Lord Wellesley's administration was altogether of a belligerent character. We had, first, a Mysore war; and as a sort of corollary, an active campaign against the fragments of the Mysore force under " Dhoondiah Khan," with subsequent operations against the Southern Polygars, and the Insurgents of Malabar. Then, the expe-

* The bloodless, but useful campaign of the late Sir James Craig on our Western frontier.

expeditions to Egypt, and the Persian Gulph; and at short intervals, two successive Marhatta wars; and, lastly, hostilities with the Rajah of Burtpore, which were not attended with our accustomed success; and such was the expense occasioned by our severe contest with the Marhatta States, that the heavy arrear * of war charge absorbed our resources for two years after its termination.

In the pacific administration of Sir G. Barlow and Lord Minto, we were compelled to set on foot a large army to quell a refractory landholder of the Doaub, (the country between the Ganges and Jumna), who, encouraged by our failure at Burtpore, defended for some time the petty forts of " *Cumouna*" and " *Girnoury*" against the utmost efforts of our arms. We sent forth, at a subsequent period, those expeditions which achieved the conquest of Java and the French islands ;

* The late Lord Lake entertained a large body of irregular troops (Asiatic " *Brabancons* "), which Lord Cornwallis on his return to India, ordered to be disbanded; but we had not the means of paying their arrears, and they could not, therefore, be immediately discharged from the service. In this dilemma, they were paid off and disbanded as funds could be obtained, and our regular army was allowed to continue in arrear. The preference given to the irregulars in regard to the discharge of arrears had the appearance of great injustice; but our troops, both European officers and sepoys, submitted with patience under great privations, and manifested an admirable temper on the occasion.

islands; and we furnished costly subsidies* and the materiel of war to our ally, the King of Persia, to enable him to contend with our other ally, the Emperor of Russia.

In Lord Hastings' government we had a Nepaul War; a Pindarry War,† and a Mahratta War; with another expedition against the pirates of the Persian Gulf; and yet, notwithstanding this almost uninterrupted series of military enterprizes, we have come forth with renewed strength, enlarging the wide circle of our dominion after every struggle.

In a season of peace the surplus revenue of India may safely 'be estimated, I think, at two millions sterling per annum, taking the year 1821-1822 as a basis for the calculation. The surplus in that year amounted to £1,927,000 sterling,

* It is somewhat singular, that we were assisting the King of Persia against the Emperor of Russia, at the same moment that we were assisting the Emperor of Russia against the late Emperor of France. This political *solecism* is not however chargeable to the Indian Government.

† If ever a war were justified on grounds of humanity, it was the Pindarry war. These freebooters, the bane, the scourge, and the opprobrium of India, have been rooted out for the time, and I am willing to hope for a very long time; and the contest, in its origin, progress, and termination, must be contemplated with sentiments of unmingled satisfaction. It was not less honourable than that which placed the British standard on the proud heights of Himmalayah.

G

sterling, at the exchange of 2s. the current rupee, and the accounts exhibit a fair specimen of the ordinary revenue and charge upon a peace establishment. The military establishments, it is true, have since been augmented, and fluctuations may be expected to take place in different branches of the revenue ; but had peace continued, a reduction of interest would have been effected in the present year to the amount of £150,000 or £200,000 per annum, by the application of from three to four millions to the extinction of debt. For estimating a larger surplus than two millions, I can perceive no safe ground whatever ; and there is quite sufficient ground for just exultation, that so ample a tribute should be drawn from a dependent territory, without impoverishing the people. This surplus, as I have before explained, is liable to a deduction to the extent of a million and a half sterling, on account of the territorial, or political charges incurred in England ; and the net territorial income of the East-India Company from British India, may, therefore, be stated, during the continuance of peace, at the sum of five hundred thousand pounds per annum.

But we are againat war. Those golden assurances have not been realised, which promised us a long continuance of peace and security. How many short months have passed since we were taught to believe that there remained no state in India which could oppose the British power; that the relations of amity had been established with all around us upon a firm and durable foundation; and that we were at length arrived at that happy epoch when we might expect to enjoy, under our vines and fig trees, the produce of all our toil, the fruits of so many victories in the field, and triumphs in the cabinet!

And are those who gave us such assurances to be condemned, because this pleasing illusion has been dispelled? certainly not—appearances justified their hopes, and seemed to countenance all the flattering anticipations which were indulged. Lord Hastings observed the same policy towards the Birman State of Ava, which Lord Minto had observed towards the Goorka State of Nepaul, and upon similar considerations. Our practice had been, in both instances, to forbear and overlook slight offences and aggressions, rather than involve ourselves in an arduous and unprofitable contest. The chain of mountains on our northern frontier, and a wild impervious jungle, or wood, on our eastern border, constituted a natural barrier, which it was not easy to penetrate, and which it was not our interest to open. A judgment may be formed of the advantage which we derived from this supposed barrier, from the fact, that a single regiment of sepoys was found sufficient for the service of

the

the extensive tract of country possessed by us to the east of the Ganges, while a force, scarcely more considerable, was considered adequate to the protection of our northern frontier from the Burrumpooter to the Gogra. Thus, nearly the whole of our military strength was concentrated in our western provinces, the most accessible part of our territory ; and we had always a disposable force which could be thrown upon any point where its service might happen to be required.

This is not the fit place for inquiring into the origin of the Burmese war, or for examining the political bearings of an event so much to be deprecated ; my present purpose is merely to notice its probable effects upon our finances ; and without pretending to furnish any accurate estimate of the war charge likely to be incurred, I may safely assume, that during the continuance of hostilities, not only will the surplus revenue be absorbed, but we must be prepared for an expenditure exceeding our ordinary income. The army employed in the field cannot be less than 30,000 men, and with the expense* of transports for the convey-

---

* Twenty thousand tons of shipping, or forty ships averaging 500 tons, will probably be required, and their freight or hire may be computed at 6000 Rupees per month each, 2,40,000 Rupees per month, or per annum Rupees 28,80,000. The excess of military charge in Bengal is estimated at Sicca Rupees 38,46,000 : that of Madras at Rupees 42,00,000. Of Bombay I cannot speak at present;

ance of the troops, military stores, and supplies necessary for their subsistence in a hostile country, the war charge may be expected to amount to from two millions to two millions and a-half per annum. Should then the contest be prolonged to a second year, the extraordinary expenditure will not probably fall short of five millions sterling, and instead of extinguishing debt in the present year 1824-25 to the amount of three millions, as contemplated, we shall probably add to the public debt of India in the course of 1825-26, the sum of one million, while the territorial account abroad and at home, will be deteriorated in the sum of four millions sterling.*

Whether any pecuniary indemnification will be found in the success of our arms, is a speculation in which it would be idle to indulge at present; all we can fairly look forward to is the speedy termi-

sent; and in fact the estimates are all likely, I think, to be exceeded, for they seldom provide sufficiently for the expenditure of military stores, and the various contingencies incidental to a state of war.

```
  * Indian peace surplus for two years....................£4,000,000
Deduct, home charge......... do. ............ £3,000,000
      War charge ......... do. ............... 5,000,000
                                            ———— 8,000,000

            Territorial deterioration...................... 4,000,000
Deduct, surplus cash balance applicable to the discharge
      of debt ..................................... 3,000,000
                                            ————
            Debt to be raised in 1825-26 ............ £1,000,000
                                            ————
```

termination of a war which it was not our interest to provoke, and which we can have no motive for prolonging beyond the necessity of the case.

Although this unexpected event will, for a time, derange all our calculations with respect to the future, I hope that the statements and explanations which I have furnished, will have satisfied the reader that the gloomy picture drawn by M. Say does not, in any of its features, represent the present financial situation of the East-India Company in India. We are neither burthened with a territorial debt of forty-eight millions, nor are we consuming the vital substance of the mother country by an annual deficit, which absorbs the produce of its labour.

I cannot, at the same time, upon a deliberate examination of the public accounts, corroborate the sanguine views and anticipations of the Marquess of Hastings. We have never had a surplus of four millions in India, and I cannot discover any sufficient ground for estimating such a revenue for the time to come ;* but we have lately realised a surplus of about two millions sterling, and we may reasonably expect to realise it again

during

---

* The revenue of the new territory will probably improve, but it will be seen in the sequel, that the receipts from the opium monopoly have already decreased, and are likely to fall off hereafter in a still greater degree. I have, also, great doubts about the stability of the land revenue of Fort St. George.

during a period of peace. Even for this sum it is,
however, extremely difficult to find a remittance
under a system of commercial regulation, which
goes far to exclude a portion of the produce and
manufactures of British India from the home market ; and if, under such circumstances, it were
in our option to extend the annual tribute to four
millions, I should not hesitate to say that considerations of policy, of justice and humanity, would
all alike concur to condemn the unmeasured
exaction. If the public revenue should unex-
pectedly become more productive, it would be
the duty of the Government to repeal or to reduce
objectionable taxes ; to increase the judicial and
other establishments, so as to render justice more
accessible to the great body of the people ; to
endow public institutions for providing better
means of education, or hospitals for the care of
the sick and the destitute ; to construct roads
and bridges, reservoirs and water-courses ; to
support caravansaries for the accommodation of
the traveller ; and otherwise to promote those
objects which may conduce to the comfort, convenience and well-being of our native subjects.
A certain revenue is required to maintain our
establishments abroad, to defray the political expenses incurred at home, and to provide a moderate fund for the gradual extinction of debt ; but
whatever may be collected beyond the fund
required

required for these several purposes, ought to be expended on the spot for the benefit of the people, whose industry supplies such ample contributions.

CHAPTER II.

SOURCES OF THE REVENUE OF INDIA—SALT—OPIUM
—CUSTOMS—ABKARRY—STAMPS, &c.

———◆———

Having submitted a brief statement of the revenue of India in the aggregate, 1 now propose to
particularize the items, or ingredients, of which it
is composed, and to consider how far our system
of taxation has been established and regulated
upon just principles, and how far we can reasonably expect that the plenteous spring which
now periodically replenishes our exchequer, will
continue to afford the same abundant supply.

From time immemorial the land has constituted
the chief source of revenue in India, and for plain
and obvious reasons. The habits of the great
body of the people are simple and uniform; their
diet is spare, and confined generally to a few articles of the first necessity, rice, vegetables, fish,
and the smaller grains ; their clothing is scanty
and mean ; their habitations poor and unfurnished ;
what we term luxuries, are confined to the opulent
few. Capital is thinly distributed over the surface,

H   and

and even the advantages of a genial climate, a prolific soil, and of manufacturing skill, were not found sufficient to swell the stream of commerce.

In all this the keen eye of the financier could see nothing to touch ; the objects were too minute and worthless, or too widely dispersed to come fairly within his grasp; and he was compelled to have recourse to the expedient of taxing produce in the *aggregate.* Such is the land tax, which, without being applied to any individual article, takes a portion of the gross produce of each particular portion of land.

As the land revenue of India is still our principal resource, I shall reserve the observations which I may have occasion to offer regarding it, until I shall have noticed the other less important branches of revenue, which will be more easily disposed of.

The *salt* stands second in point of importance; and, as it has been so often stigmatized under the reproachful term " monopoly," it will be proper to bestow a little attention upon the principles on which this tax has been established.

If a certain revenue be required beyond what the land will produce ; and if the number of opulent consumers, in whose hands luxuries, and other tangible objects of taxation, might be found, be so small and so dispersed that the charge of collection would go far to absorb the produce of the

tax, then it would appear that a government has
no alternative but to have recourse to some article
of general consumption as the object of taxation.
It never can answer any useful purpose to teaze
and torment a country with taxes and tax-ga-
therers, when such taxes are unproductive, or
produce little more than is sufficient to maintain
a host of revenue officers. These officers are an
evil in any country; but in India, where it is
almost impossible to prevent their mal-practices,
they are a serious evil. Such is the force of long
established habit under a bad government, that,
even now, when there is an anxiety felt by the
ruling power to repress abuse and to afford protection to all, the revenue officer exacts, and the
people suffer his exaction, as a matter of course,
and almost without a complaint.

If, again, a people be constitutionally timid, or
unable, from whatever cause, to defend their property and to resist oppression, then it would seem
to be a happy discovery, if, instead of subjecting
them by direct taxation to the screw of the Exchequer, the government should succeed in drawing from them the periodical contribution required,
by a process scarcely perceptible, in sums so
minute as scarcely to be felt, and by means totally
divested of the odious character of *force.*

I will not say that these were the considerations
which led to the establishment of the salt mono-

H 2   poly ;

poly; but they are the considerations which may be urged to justify it. The government have selected it as an article of general consumption, which can be rendered productive ; and as a medium or instrument, for levying contributions, by a sort of voluntary process, without the intervention of the tax-gatherer. It approaches, I own, to a poll tax ; but it is a very light poll tax, which is paid almost insensibly : and where, as in India, the great mass of the people, with few exceptions, are in nearly the same condition, there is no injustice, and little inequality in applying to them one common scale of taxation, regulated by the scale of their consumption.

In Bengal the manufacture of salt is a strict monopoly, and the article is not allowed to be imported, even from the coast of Coromandel and other parts of *our own territory,* except on account of Government, or under *"permits"* from Government, requiring its delivery into the public stores at a stipulated price.

The manufacture is carried on in Bengal throughout the districts which skirt the Delta of the Ganges, on low lands periodically overflowed by the spring tides ; and as it is confined to as narrow a tract as possible, smuggling may be sufficiently guarded against. The zemindars, or landholders, in whose estates it was found convenient to establish the manufacture, were allowed
compen-

compensation for the lands which were appropriated to the purpose, (" *kalary* rents," as they are termed); and this compensation was generally, I believe, regulated on fair and equitable terms.

But, heretofore, the manufacture was the source of great misery to the inhabitants of the adjacent districts, who were often forced into the service, and compelled to expose themselves in the unhealthy marshes of the sunderbunds, to the attacks of tigers and alligators, and to all the physical ills engendered by a pestilential climate. This grievance has, I trust, been removed; we have established courts of justice to protect all our native subjects, and the wretched Molungees among the rest; recourse is no longer had to compulsory service; from one of the most objectionable stations the manufacture was long since withdrawn; the advance of cultivation, by gradually diminishing the jungle, may be expected to render the country more healthy; and as the Molungees are generally natives of the districts in which they are now employed, they are not so liable to suffer from the effects of the climate. But still these Molungees are, I fear, among the worst conditioned of our subjects; and the necessity for employing men in situations where they may become the victims of ferocious animals and disease, forms, in my opinion, the greatest objection to the salt monopoly. This objection it would
be

be idle to urge, if there were no alternative, for men will have salt at whatever risk or sacrifice it may be obtained ; and if the Government should decline to supply the article, it would be manufactured by private individuals ; but in point of fact, there is an alternative, which is not liable to the same objections : salt can be manufactured in almost any quantity on the neighbouring coast of Coromandel, under a warmer sun, in a drier atmosphere, and with every circumstance of advantage ; and it appears to me that we should consult both the interests of the revenue and the interests of humanity, by a partial transfer at least of the salt manufacture from some of our Bengal districts to those of the northern sircars.

The following statement will shew the produce of the salt sales in Bengal, and the cost and charges of manufacture in the last fourteen years, or from 1808-9.

	Gross Sale.	Cost and Charge.
1808-9 ...	Ct. Rs. 1,82,69,505 ...	Ct. Rs. 40,45,276
1809-10	1,77,14,711	42,36,073
1810-11	1,72,27,019	41,24,303
1811-12	1,81,47,129	49,00,001
1812-13	1,67,46,642	60,76,677
1813-14	1,77,86,141	65,11,578
1814-15	1,56,86,433	42,58,169
1815-16	1,60,04,989	39,05,288
1816-17	1,71,31,682	47,61,455
1817-18	1,86,71,974	48,77,123

1818-

	Gross Sale.	Cost and Charges.
1818-19...	Ct. Rs. 1,85,03,785 ...	Ct. Rs. 54,32,192
1819-20	1,90,27,939	60,23,041
1820-12	1,90,35,117	56,65,408
1821-22	2,06,07,680	59,71,710

The quantity of salt sold within the year was
formerly from 40 to 45,00,000 maunds, but it
has been gradually increased, and of late years
the sales have been extended to 48,00,000 maunds.
The selling prices varied heretofore from 320 to
*350 sicca rupees the 100 maunds; but the
average has been higher of late, and at the March
and May sales of 1822 the article reached the exorbitant price of Sicca Rupees 437. 1. 2. at the
former, and Sicca Rupees 593. 14. 7. at the latter
sale. This is much too high an average, for when
the article attains this price the tax is really felt
as a grievance by the people, whose simple diet
requires the addition of salt as a stimulant. When
the

* The average of 1821-22 was Sicca Rupees 358 2 6 per 100
maunds. When reference is made to the Bengal accounts it is necessary to quote the *Sicca* Rupee, in which those accounts are kept.
In the English accounts, the *Current* Rupee is used, and in quoting
from them, I think it right to give that rupee, for my statements
could not otherwise be verified. The Current Rupee is a nominal
value, used to bring the different coins of India to one common
standard; but I should be glad to see it altogether disused. The
Sicca is as 100 to 116 of the Current Rupee. The latter is easily
converted into English money, being valued by the Company at two
shillings. The pound sterling is therefore arrived at by taking one-
tenth.

the average exceeds 350 rupees the 100 maunds, the quantity at the public sales should be augmented ; and by retaining a sufficient stock of the article and supplying the market according to circumstances, it is very much in the power of the Government to regulate the price to the consumer, who will not complain while it does not exceed 350 rupees per 100 maunds. Taking the consumption of the Bengal provinces east of Benares, in which the Bengal salt is chiefly consumed, at 45,00,000 maunds, and the population at thirty millions, the inhabitants will consume annually, on a medium, six seers per head, which at 350 sicca rupees per 100 maunds will cost about $12\frac{1}{2}d$. to each individual ; of this fourpence may be considered the natural price of the article, being the cost of production, and the remaining $8\frac{1}{2}d$. is the tax received by Government. This sum,* insignificant as it may appear, would not be a very trifling contribution from the lowest classes of India ; but as these do not consume at the rate of the general average, they do not pay quite so much. The opulent few, with their families and numerous retainers, consume upon a more liberal scale

* The people of Great Britain contribute in taxes at the rate of about £3. per head on a medium. The people of India at about 5s. per head (or 1-12th of that rate); but I am disposed to think that the latter are, nevertheless, more heavily assessed than the former, regard being had to their respective means of paying taxes.

scale of allowance ; and salt is supplied also in some instances to the cattle.

But, although I have endeavoured to justify the principle of the tax, or, rather, the necessity which exists in India for levying the public contributions from articles of general consumption, I am very far from justifying its immoderate extension. Our object ought to be to draw our present income from a larger quantity ; for it is unquestionable that the people do not consume as much salt as they desire to use, and we certainly have it in our power to place the article more within their reach, and to afford them a more liberal measure of indulgence, without any sacrifice of the present revenue.

Benares, and the territory west and north of that province, are supplied with rock salt, and other salts from the country beyond the Jumna : and soon after our acquisition of what are called " the Ceded and Conquered Provinces," an attempt was made to draw a revenue from the monopoly of the salt which is imported from Malwa, Lahore, and other districts lying beyond our own frontier. The experiment, however, failed, and was abandoned, not one moment sooner than was desirable ; for it was undertaken without due attention to circumstances. The manufacture was not in our own hands; and it was impossible to prevent the introduction of

I the

the article into our provinces, where the price
had been artificially raised far beyond its natural
level, without employing an army of custom-
house officers, who would have been a pest to
the country. The project was also injudicious
on another ground, since it tended to check a
barter trade between our territory and the districts west of the Jumna, which was found highly
beneficial to both parties.

At the Presidency of Fort St. George, a revenue is, also, drawn from salt, which, in the year
1821-22, amounted to current rupees 31,85,763 ;
but I am not aware that any useful purpose
would be answered by entering into further details on this subject.

In concluding it, I may observe, that the salt
revenue is one of the branches of our Indian
resources, upon whose stability and permanency
we can most confidently rely ; and, although I
do not pretend to maintain that it is free from
all objections, I consider it less objectionable
and less injurious in its effects than some other
taxes which we have imposed ; and while the
present revenue is required, the mere circumstance of its bearing an unpopular designation
ought not to prejudice us against it, or to induce
us to give it up for the purpose of substituting a
system of taxation, more consistent with European theory, but at the same time, much more
likely

likely to expose our Asiatic subjects to exactions and to personal oppression.

THE OPIUM MONOPOLY.

This. branch of revenue is associated in character with the salt monopoly, and naturally follows it, although, in other respects, it is not entitled to take precedence of the customs. In principle, the two monoplies bear a close resemblance; but there are circumstances which distinguish them. The salt is a tax levied upon our own subjects; the opium is a tax levied upon the people of China and the inhabitants of the Eastern Archipelago. Salt, if not an absolute necessary of life; is highly conducive to comfort and health. Opium, except when used as a medicine, is an intoxicating drug; hence, the object should be in the one instance to draw the same revenue from the largest possible quantity; in the other, to draw the same revenue from the smallest possible quantity; and experience has shewn in the case of opium, that the amount of revenue is in general inversely as the quantity sold. In fact, we have found (fortunately for the character of our morals) that 4,000 chests of that article will yield a larger produce than 5,000 chests.

ɪ 2   The

The manufacture of opium in Bengal is a strict monopoly, and I have to vindicate this tax against the same prejudices, which the very term " *monopoly*" never fails to excite ; but, although I cannot, in a manner quite satisfactory to myself, get over one objection to which the monopoly is liable, namely, that the government have been compelled, as a means of securing it, to prohibit the cultivation of the poppy in particular districts, and thus to trench upon the rights of property ; yet, even for this stretch of power, some excuse may be found, since the general use of an intoxicating drug is not only productive of physical evil, but is, moreover, calculated to have a prejudicial effect upon the morals and good order of society.

In other respects, I have no formidable difficulty to surmount. When strictly examined, the tax on opium will be found to resolve itself into a high export duty, which is paid by the foreign consumer, and which is regulated by the exporting merchant, who determines the price to be paid for the article upon his own view of what the foreign consumer can, or will, pay for it.

The opium costs the Company in Bengal from 225 to 250 rupees per chest :* it is exposed to public sale, periodically, under an express stipulation

* The chest contains two factory maunds—149½ lbs.

lation that the article shall be exported. The merchant bids for it what he pleases ; sometimes more and sometimes less : there is free competition, and the difference between the actual cost of the article and the sale price, is evidently nothing more nor less than a custom-house duty. Wherein would be the difference, if the Government disposed of the opium at prime cost, or allowed others to manufacture it, and afterwards imposed a duty of 100 or 1,000 per cent. on the exportation of the article ? The existing system is, no doubt, to be preferred, because it is better calculated to prevent smuggling, and because the exporting merchant is better qualified to determine the proper rate of duty than the Government can pretend to be.

High rates of customs may have a prejudicial effect in checking exportation ; but in this instance the tax is paid *voluntarily*, and does not prevent exportation. The Chinese are certainly made to pay very high for our opium ; and they in return make us pay very high for their teas : but we scarcely can be said to do them an injury by raising the price, so as to discourage the use of a drug, which, however excellent as a medicine, cannot be used habitually, or in excess, without injury to the individual who indulges in the habit.

Prior

Prior to the administration of Lord Teignmouth, the opium revenue was of small account.
The article was provided by contract : the drug
was in general impure ; it was not held in esti-
mation in the foreign market ; and so late as the
year 1797-8, it averaged only Sicca Rupees 414. 15.
per chest. In the following year 1798-9, the
price rose to Sicca Rupees 775. 3. per chest : it
continued to rise from that time, fluctuating,
however, at particular periods, until in 1822-23
it averaged 3,090 Sicca Rupees per chest ;* the
quantity brought to sale in that year, being only
3,504 chests, or 1,000 chests below the quantity
usually disposed of by the Government.

The improvement in the revenue is, in a very
great degree, to be ascribed to the change in
the system of management introduced by Lord
Teignmouth. The contracts were abolished ;
the opium was provided by public agents, to
whom a liberal commission was granted on the
sales ; the manufacture was confined to the districts most favourable to the growth of the
poppy ; a rigid examination was established at
the Presidency to insure the purity of the drug ;
its quality was rapidly improved ; the confidence
of the exporting merchant and foreign consumer
was gradually secured ; and, in the course of a
few

* It has averaged as high as Sicca Rupees 4,001. 4. 11. per chest.

few years, a chest of opium, bearing the Company's marks, passed among the Malays and Chinese like a bank-note, unexamined and unquestioned.

The quantity of the article annually brought to sale in Calcutta, has been from 4,000 to 4,500 chests, 2,500 of which were understood to be consumed in China ; while about 2,000 chests were distributed among the inhabitants of Java, Sumatra, Borneo, Celebes, and the other islands in the Eastern Seas. Four thousand five hundred chests were heretofore supposed to be the largest quantity which could be disposed of with advantage ; and although the consumption has probably increased, and is increasing, there are strong grounds for believing that we shall not consult the interests of the revenue by extending the sales beyond that quantity.

The following statement will shew the gross produce of the sales of Bengal opium during the last 14 years, or from 1808-9, with the cost and charges of manufacture, *viz.*

	Gross Receipts.	Cost and Charges.
1808-9	*Current*Rs. 59,56,354	*Current* Rs. 9,67,278
1809-10	82,23,431	8,31,275
1810-11	93,59,961	9,61,879
1811-12	92,46,775	8,77,325
1812 13	72,99,401	8,80,528
1813-14	96,40,729	10,77,638
1814 15	1,10,35,626	8,29,881

1815-

	Gross Receipts.	Costs and Charges.
1815-16	...Ct. Rs. 1,05(12,601...	Ct. Rs. 10,97,585
1816-17	94,16,539 .'	11,85,490
1817-18	87,35,983	8,92,496
1818-19	83,05,846	8,89,915
1819-20	79,98,248	10,35,066
1820-21	1,43,64,321	13,57,259
1821-22	1,12,57,275	9,86,722

It will appear, from this statement, that, although the revenue has fluctuated from time to time, it has been in a course of progressive advancement, and I have been accustomed to consider the opium as one of those branches of our Indian revenue upon whose stability and improvement we could most confidently rely. Very different views have, however, been lately adopted with respect to the means of encreasing this resource ; and I am led to apprehend that the change of plan will not only fail to produce the advantages expected, but that it will have the effect of rendering the existing revenue extremely precarious.

In the province of Malwa, and other districts on the western side of India, opium had long been produced, and had found its way, through various indirect channels, into China and the other markets in the Indian Seas, interfering, more or less, with the sale of our Bengal produce.

When this territory came into our possession by the successful termination of the Mahratta

War in 1818, the government appear to have adopted the notion that a field was opened for extending the opium monopoly ; and departing at once from the maxim, heretofore acted upon, of circumscribing the produce and of confining the manufacture to particular districts, supposed to be most favourably situated for the growth of the poppy, they made large advances for its cultivation in Malwa, paid high prices for the drug, and otherwise held out every encouragement to the extension of the manufacture. Nor has this new course of policy been restricted in its application to the new territory. The government of Bengal have more recently taken measures for increasing the produce in the districts under that Presidency ; they have even appointed the *collectors of the land revenue* to act as deputies to the opium agent, and have stimulated their exertions to favour the cultivation of the poppy by granting them a commission, or per centage, on any increase which may be made to the produce. In short, without entering into the reasoning which led to the change, it will be sufficient to state that it is now broadly maintained that our object should be to *encourage production,* and to draw a revenue upon a larger quantity, which, being disposed of at moderate prices, may be expected to check foreign competition, and not only to secure, but to enlarge, the markets of consumption. The article

K   is

is also supplied for our own domestic occasions, and there seems to be no longer any intention to discourage the use of the drug by our native subjects ; although, heretofore, the utmost precaution was observed to prevent their obtaining it, even in the smallest quantity.

In the instance of salt and tea, I concur entirely in the position, that we should endeavour to raise a moderate revenue upon a large consumption ; but in the case of opium, a different policy should, I think, be pursued. I do not mean to affirm that the quantity may not be too small and the prices too high ; because very high prices operate as a premium, which promotes smuggling and adulteration, as well as foreign* competition ; but as far as it can be circumscribed *without* producing such effects, it is desirable, I think, that it should be limited. The accounts printed for Parliament do not shew the number of chests brought to sale annually by the government, or it would, I believe, appear that, in almost every instance, the proceeds of those sales have been nearly in the inverse ratio of the quantity disposed of ; and, with this evidence before us, it is surely not

* The cultivation of the poppy has, I understand, been successfully introduced into the Philippine Islands, which are placed in the very centre of the opium consumers; and I am apprehensive that our sales will be affected by a competition from this quarter.

not wise or prudent to extend the manufacture unnecessarily.

The following memorandum will shew the progress which has been made in realizing an opium revenue from Malwa, in the two first years of the experiment.

	Gross Receipts. Current Rupees.	Advance and Charges. Current Rupees.
1820-21.............		 3,23,347
1821-22.............	33,89,333	41,99,741
	Per Estimate.	Per Estimate.
1822-23.............	32,12,500	65,60,600

Here we have a very heavy *charge* in lieu of a *revenue*; but 1 do not mean to say that this is a just exhibition of the ultimate result. The large advances which have been made (most improvidently, as I conceive) have produced, and will produce, opium, more than sufficient, probably, to replace the disbursement; but I have reason to know that we are going on with our advances upon a very large scale, and I see reason to apprehend, not only that the proceeds of the sales of Malwa opium will do little more than reimburse the cost of the article, but that those sales will, in a very material degree, affect the sale of our Bengal produce.

When we advert, moreover, to the magnitude of the sum advanced for the article in Malwa, in 1822-23, it is impossible not to feel a little startled:

it

it is more than six times the amount paid for the whole produce of Bengal (about 4,500 chests); and we must conclude, either that we are to obtain six times the quantity, or that we are to pay six times the price for the Malwa opium, or that both quantity and price are to be augmented. The latter is the true supposition : we are to pay much more than the natural price or cost of production in Bengal ; and this most powerful stimulant is to be applied to obtain an article which we do not want. We place an enormous sum in the hands of an agent, so far removed from the seat*

of

* This, in itself, is one among many strong reasons for establishing a separate Government in " Central India," or in some convenient situation west of the Jumna. Sir John Malcolm has warmly recommended the measure, and I entirely concur in its expediency. Our connections and interests have become so multifarious and complicated in that quarter that they require constant and vigilant attention. A spark which might be extinguished at the moment by a Government on the spot, may rise into a flame before a reference can be made to the distant Presidency of Fort William—and surrounded as we are by Marhattahs—Affghans—Rajapoots—Sikhs—Jaats—and other tribes, having dissimilar views and interests, such sparks must frequently be elicited. Seventeen years ago my colleague and myself, when employed as a Board of Commissioners for the settlement of the Ceded and Conquered Provinces, " urged the expediency of a responsible and respectable administration being established in that distant and valuable territory ;" but the necessity for it is become much more urgent and apparent, now that we have extended our frontier to the west, and that the attention of the Supreme Government has unfortunately been called by a new enemy to the *east*. See Report from Commissioners, printed in the " Revenue Selections," pages 6 to 44.

of Government as to be beyond all efficient controul ; and the credit of that officer is to depend, in a great measure, upon his exertions to produce an excessive quantity of a deleterious drug ! If the money thus expended found its way to the cultivators of the soil, or to the village zemindars, who would return a part in the shape of rent or revenue, there would be less to regret ; but is this the case ? Some of the native chiefs may receive a portion of the amount ; but a portion by no means inconsiderable is likely, I fear, to be engrossed by contractors, native officers, intermediate agents, and others, whom it cannot be the interest of the Government to maintain and encourage.

Two reasons may be assigned for the late proceeding of the Government of India : the one, that they could not, with justice to the landholders, suppress the cultivation of the poppy in our new territory ; the other, that we could not prevent the opium, which is produced in the territories of the native chiefs, who enjoy a real or nominal independence, from finding its way through clandestine channels to the sea-coast, and from thence to the markets of consumption.

The former reason is plausible, and I am no advocate for interfering with the free use of property ; but we ought to be consistent : we peremptorily suppressed the cultivation of the
poppy

poppy in the Bengal districts of Rungpore, Purneah, and Baugulpore, where it had been grown for ages, and where a permanent settlement of the revenue had been concluded with the landholders, limiting the public demand, and recognizing all the rights of property on their part; and yet we hesitate about doing the same thing in places where it had not been cultivated before, where no settlement has been made, and where, consequently, it is open to the Government to make any arrangements they may think proper with the occupants of the soil. Is not this to strain at the knat after having swallowed the camel? The proceeding in Bengal was arbitrary; but some excuse may be found for it, if, in addition to the desire naturally felt to preserve an important branch of revenue, the Government was influenced by considerations having reference to objects of police.

The second reason appears to me to be quite unsatisfactory and inconclusive. It is surely more easy for us to prevent the illicit manufacture and exportation of opium, now that nearly the whole of central and western India is under our direct authority or subject to our influence, than it was when this territory was held by independent and even hostile states. Malwa opium was always exported to a certain extent, from the western side of India, and a small quantity might still find

its

its way to the sea through the Portuguese ports of Diu and Damaun, but it would be in our power to render that quantity very small, and its price very high, either by the imposition of high transit duties, or by declaring the article *contraband*. This is not an expedient perfectly satisfactory to the mind ; but the principle and the practice are recognised and have been long enforced by the enlightened Government of Great Britain, against those fearful articles, French lace, China crape, and Indian brocades.

Under these circumstances we must, I fear, look for the true explanation of our measures, in the desire felt by the Government to establish in Malwa the same profitable monopoly which we have succeeded in establishing in Bengal ; but I apprehend that the expectation will be disappointed. Whether the monopoly in itself be justifiable or not in principle, it is not for me to decide ; but viewed only as an instrument of taxation, I must contend that the means which have lately been pursued for its extension, are calculated to produce effects the very reverse of those contemplated, and that far from looking to any improvement, the experiment, if persevered in for two or three years, will end in the destruction of the present revenue.*

Another

* The receipts in 1822-23 and 1823-24 will, however, be very large, as there was an arrear outstanding of Sicca Rupees 34,76,000,

on

Another disadvantage has attended our operations in Malwa : under the very judicious arrangements which had been for some time in operation, a considerable gain by exchange had been derived by the Government, on the very large supplies annually furnished from Bengal in aid of the limited resources of Bombay ; but in consequence of the enormous sum required for the provision of the Malwa opium, the agent has been allowed to negotiate bills on Calcutta and its dependencies, to an extent exceeding what the trade could supply : his bills have come into competition with those of the Bombay Government, and instead of gaining, as heretofore, a difference of exchange of not less than eight per cent., a loss is likely now to be sustained on our remittances to the western parts of India.

Every thing had been so well regulated that the Government of India gained invariably upon almost all its exchange transactions, and the difference of exchange had become no insignificant source of income; but I observe, with regret, that even our remittances to China have not of late

on the 30th April 1822, and the prices continued high in 1822-23. They have now fallen, and will, I fear, continue to fall. The revenue of 1824-5 from the Bengal opium is not expected to exceed Sicca Rupees 72,00,000 on Rupees 56,70,000 below the actual receipts of 1822-23; and even this reduced revenue will not be realized, if we continue to encourage the production of opium in Malwa.

late been effected with the same advantage as heretofore. In the course of the last year a large remittance was made from Calcutta to Canton in specie ; but as it was composed of the coins of Bengal (the Spanish dollar not being procurable probably in sufficient quantity), and as those coins would not answer the purposes of the supra-cargoes, the money has been sent back through a private house of business, and a loss is likely to be sustained by the Company in freight, insurance (or risk), interest, and the charges of agency, to the extent of not less than ten or twelve per cent. The very circumstance of the supra-cargoes calling for a remittance in specie, shews that the exchange had fallen, or was expected to fall, and the fact is corroborated by late advices from Canton.

Sayer, or Excise, including the Abkarry, or Tax on Spirituous Liquors and intoxicating Drugs.

The sayer will be taken next in order, as the abkarry, which constitutes the principal branch of it, bears some affinity to the tax on opium in one of its features.

The abkarry was established by us upon a regular footing, partly with a view to objects of police, and partly for the purpose of drawing a revenue, at the same time that we discouraged and checked the bad habits of our native subjects.

L   It

It was imagined that we should diminish the use
of fermented liquors and drugs, by rendering the
article more expensive to the consumer; and
that we should, also, by licensing the shops for its
sale, have it in our power to maintain a more
effectual controul over the haunts of depredators
and other ill disposed persons, accustomed to
disturb the peace and good order of society.

In both these speculations we have, I fear,
been disappointed, and had we looked a little
deeper into human nature, we might, perhaps,
originally have come to a different conclusion.
The use of spirituous liquors and drugs by the
natives has increased, and is still increasing, and
with it, I apprehend, their vices. In India, habits
of intoxication are not regarded as they are in
some other countries, with indulgence and even
favour ; they are revolting to all the feelings of the
people, and to all their notions of propriety ; and
the Hindoo, who once addicts himself to drinking,
must be content to take a very low place in the
scale of society : in truth, the practice prevails
only among the lower orders both of Hindoos and
Mussulmans ; and if a few individuals at the
opposite extremity of the scale should addict
themselves to it, the gratification is indulged in
private, for no person, at all scrupulous about character, would expose himself to the certainty of
forfeiting the esteem of his countrymen by pub-
licly

licly manifesting a disregard of all their feelings and prejudices.

In the Hindoo Zemindary of Nuddeah I have heard that not a single shop existed until we licensed the vend of spirituous liquors and drugs; and at present not a village in it could probably be pointed out, in which such a shop would not be found. Men used spirits, no doubt, in former times, and the lowest classes largely in some places; but while they did so in private, the evil did not extend so far. The license of government gave a sort of public sanction to the practice, and the disgrace incurred by individuals, was diminished by being participated with their rulers. The increase which has taken place in the Abkarry, is not perhaps in itself sufficient to justify me in asserting that habits of intoxication have become more generally prevalent; but such is the received opinion, and it is quite certain that among the Hindoos, such habits must have a very prejudicial effect upon the morals and social condition of that people.

It was, also, I fear, a miscalculation to assume that the police could exercise a more efficient superintendence over persons of bad character, in consequence of our licensing " Public Houses." The " *Abkars*," or publicans, are themselves people of very low caste and condition in India; it is their interest to have customers, and they would

not

not long retain customers if they habitually betrayed them. Public houses are the usual resort of the idle and dissolute, and a convenient rendezvous for those who meditate felonious designs which must be executed by the concert of numbers. Drinking is often the prelude, and the incentive to their crimes ; men drink that they may rob, and rob that they may drink : gaming, if not a kindred vice, is not unfrequently associated with drinking; and both exercise a baneful influence by inflaming the passions, by lowering the tone of character, and rendering the fortunes of men desperate.

It was equally a miscalculation to assume that the use of spirituous liquors would be diminished by enhancing the price of the article by means of taxation. The materials for intoxication are everywhere to be found in India, at so cheap a rate, that the duty can produce no sensible effect. If it be moderate, it will not be felt; if it be very high, it can be, and will be, evaded.

What then remains to be done ? Can we retrace our steps ? I fear not, for when a habit is once established among a people, it is extremely difficult to eradicate it. We could not now, without great violence, abolish our abkarry system ; but we might have refrained from supplying (as we have done lately) a large quantity of opium for our domestic consumption, since this article is a
powerful

powerful ingredient in the different preparations which are made for producing intoxication.

The abkarry will probably continue to increase; but it is, I think, to be regretted that it was ever made an object of revenue by the British Government.

I shall only notice, and that very slightly, one other branch of the sayer, or excise; I mean the duty levied on pilgrims resorting to the temples of Jagurnath, Gya, and other places.

This tax does not harmonize, I think, with the character of a great and liberal government; and our interference in the internal management of the temple at Jagurnath, can scarcely be considered judicious or respectable. It was intended, however, to prevent fraud and imposition, and to guard the pilgrims against violence and extortion; but such interference has not been found necessary at Gya, and, if not necessary, it is undoubtedly to be avoided: I own, at the same time, that, although wishing to see the tax abolished, I cannot enter into the feelings of some worthy persons in this country, who regard it with as much horror, as if they were the identical Hindoos who are the immediate objects of it.

I may observe, generally, in this place, that an excise* is not suited to the situation and habits of
the

* The sayer gungeaut, abolished by Lord Cornwallis, was a species of excise to which the natives had been long familiarized, but it was
a vexa

the people of India. It requires a multiplicity of officers for its collection ; these officers, receiving very small allowances, cannot be depended upon ; personal oppression would often be committed; the power of visiting dwelling-houses is everywhere odious: but, in India, where the female apartments cannot be entered without inflicting disgrace, such a power would be viewed with horror and detestation, and might be exercised to effect the worst purposes. Moreover, commodities which, might be judged proper objects of the excise, are found in such scanty quantity, or so widely dispersed, that a revenue could not be drawn from them without entailing a charge quite disproportionate, nor without subjecting the people to grievous vexations.

Tobacco is an article which promised better than any other, because it is one of general consumption ; and several projects have, at different times, been entertained for subjecting it to an excise ; but

---

a vexatious imposition. It consisted of duties levied in gunges, hauts, and bazaars (fairs, markets, &c.), on the sale of all commodities, partly as rent and partly to defray the expense of providing sheds, stalls, and other accommodations. One disadvantage attended the abolition ; the gunges were neglected and fell into decay, and buyers and sellers, who have an interest in meeting together, being deprived of the accustomed accommodations, did not resort to those places so generally as heretofore. The " rahdarry," or transit duty, was very properly abolished as vexatious and injurious to commerce.

but the objections to which I have adverted, were considered to be decisive against it, although I have learnt, with regret, that the project of taxing it, has lately been resumed. It is an article which is usually grown in garden-ground, adjoining the habitations of the natives ; and as they can thus supply themselves at their very doors, it could not be brought under an excise without a heavy expense, nor without subjecting the growers and consumers to an inquisitorial power, which would be perfectly intolerable.

Attempts have been made to introduce some other taxes of an objectionable character, (the house tax, shop tax, &c.) ; but as they were found to be unpopular, the good sense and proper feeling of the Goverment induced them to give way, and to withdraw the obnoxious impost, before it produced, as it threatened to do, a serious ferment and popular commotion.

THE STAMPS.

This is a tax of European origin, and little suitable to the character and habits of our native subjects. It is very expensive in collection (one of the tests of a bad tax); it is extremely vexatious, and it holds out great temptations to fraud from the ease with which the stamps can be imitated,

imitated, and from the ignorance of the people who are compelled to use them.

This immoral tendency ought especially to be guarded against in fiscal legislation, for, although the individual who will evade a tax, or defraud the revenue with little scruple, will not always defraud his neighbour, it is dangerous to shake the moral principle, since men who begin by committing what they consider (however erroneously) *venial* trespasses, are decidedly on a road which may conduct them to more serious offences. A tax, moreover, which can be easily evaded operates injuriously towards the fair dealer; and a tax which admits of impositions upon the ignorant and unwary, by throwing doubts over all contracts and commercial transactions, is liable to very serious objections.

The stamps, too, were superadded to other taxes : the individual who had to pay customs was called upon at the same time to pay for a stamp ; he who had to deposit a judicial fee on entering his suit, was also required to add to it the price of a stamp. Now, one direct tax is surely enough at a time ; and it certainly tended little to the credit of our Government to send away an ignorant native, several miles perhaps, in search of a stamp, before he was allowed to present a petition. This ground of reproach has, I believe, been removed.

This

The stamp duties made little progress for several years after their institution, but they have lately advanced more rapidly ; and if we could be satisfied that their increase is fairly to be ascribed to the increasing wealth of the people, and not to the imposition of higher rates, to their extension to new objects, or to the stricter enforcement of revenue laws, there would be something to reconcile us to the continuance of the tax. The following is a memorandum of the receipts and charges in the last three years.

BENGAL STAMP DUTIES.

	Receipts.	Charges.
1819-20	Ct. Rs. 14,61,280	Ct. Rs. 6,51,610
1820-21	15,08,971	6,51,446
1821-22	*15,14,992	6,16,916

Per Estimate.

1822-23	21,57,600	5,80,000

FORT

* In Account No. 1, page 6, of the last printed statements (bearing date May 1824) the stamps in 1821-22 are stated at *Current* Rupees 15,14,992 : and in Account No. 9, page 22, of the same series of statements, they are stated at *Sicca* Rupees 18,40,843, or *Current* Rupees 21,35,377. This difference arises from the omission of the Stamp Revenue of the " Ceded and Conquered Provinces " in Account No. 1, which is prepared in this country. It would, however, in my opinion, have been much better if the Bengal arrangement had been adhered to: 1st. Because the whole Stamp Revenue appears in one sum in the Bengal account, whereas in the English

M   account

FORT ST. GEORGE STAMP DUTIES.

	Receipts.	Charges.
1819-20 ...	Pagodas 1,29,797	... Pagodas 8,909
1820-21	1,55,607	24,379
1821-22	1,61,859	24,801

Per Estimate.

| 1822-23 | 1,43,916 | 21,235 |

BOMBAY STAMP DUTIES.

1819-20	Rupees 1,59,717	
1820-21	1,42,898	
1821-22	1,79,026	Charge not particularized in the printed accounts.

Per Estimate.

| 1822-23 | 1,65,000 | |

It will immediately strike those who have given attention to the principles of taxation, that the high rate of charge, which in Bengal has hitherto absorbed a large portion of the collections, constitutes a great objection to the stamp duties. It is improvident in any Government to take £15 from

account we can only discover a part, the remainder being incorporated with the Land Revenue. 2dly. Because in the English account *a part* of the revenue stands opposed to the *whole* charge, unless, indeed, the charge of the stamps in " the Ceded and Conquered Provinces " be also incorporated (which is not probable) with the charge of the Land Revenue; and, lastly, because the two accounts ought to be made to correspond, unless there be some strong reason for a deviation, which assuredly cannot be alleged in the present instance. Such discrepancies produce doubt, whereas the Company's accounts are entitled generally to the fullest confidence, for they are prepared by men of high character and great professional knowledge.

from the pockets of the subject, when only £9 of the amount* comes into the public exchequer; and although it would appear from the estimate of 1822-23, that the disproportion of the charge to the revenue is expected to be less hereafter, I cannot bring myself to regard the stamps as an economical tax, nor as one which can be considered free from other objections.

THE CUSTOMS.

It is gratifying always when we find the customs prosperous and improving, because from their healthful condition we may generally infer that the bounteous gifts of nature, and the works of human industry and skill, are freely distributed among the sons of man. Their productiveness is also in general an indication of wisdom and moderation on the part of the Government, for it rarely

---

* Receipts in 1821-22, say in round numbers 15,00,000
    Deduct charge .... ditto 6,00,000

                        Net Revenue 9,00,000

The charge of 6,00,000 on 9,00,000 is equal to 66⅔ per cent. But I suspect (as intimated in the preceding note) that the sum of 6,00,000, is the *total charge* upon the *total revenue* of Current Rupees 21,35,377, and, in this case, the rate of charge will be reduced to about 28 per cent.

rarely happens that excessive duties produce a large revenue.

The great secret of finance is to promote *circulation* and *consumption*; for although in the natural order of things *production* must *precede* consumption, it is quite certain that if consumers be found, and no interruptions to the circulation of commodities be interposed, production will take place. But what avails it to France that the banks of the Seine are covered with the fruits of her vineyards, if they cannot find a purchaser? Her light wines, however grateful they would be to the taste of our people, are nearly excluded from this country by disproportionate duties, and this interdiction virtually excludes from France our hardware, our beautiful cottons, and other articles, which would be highly appreciated by her population. *We* cannot urge the plea of having rival manufactures to protect, for throughout the wide extent of our dominion we do not make a single hogshead of wine from the juice of the grape, except at the Cape of Good Hope. France *has* cotton manufactures, but our capital and our machinery would enable us to supply a part of her large consumption with advantage to both parties, if we were content to receive her wines in exchange. As the dawn of a more liberal policy has lately appeared in our councils, we may indulge

indulge a hope that the experiment* will be made, and that commercial interests, which are always favourable to peace, will tend to check hereafter those military and political feelings, which have so often involved the two countries in unprofitable warfare. The manufactures of India have had to struggle of late years against desperate odds, and the powers of machinery threaten soon to annihilate them altogether. It would be idle in the people of that country to complain of the introduction of machinery, which must be regarded as one of the great improvements of the age, and it would be not less so to attempt to counteract its effects by bounties and protecting duties, even if India possessed the power to legislate for herself. But our Indian subjects have just cause to complain of being treated as *aliens* in our system of commercial policy ; and if the stream of wealth which has flowed into the mother country should become languid, or altogether fail, it will be no more than, the natural result of those restrictive measures which seem to say, "*you shall not produce, either for our benefit or your own.*" The people of India are British subjects, and they have claims

to

* Since these pages were written, the Chancellor of the Exchequer has proposed a large reduction in the duties on French wines, and I congratulate him and the country on the wisdom of the measure.

to something beyond the privilege of paying twenty-two millions sterling in annual revenue.

The Government abroad has always been attentive to the interests of commerce, and has been solicitous to promote the external trade of the country. The customs, both on imports and exports, are moderate, seldom exceeding five per cent. *ad valorem,* with double rates on foreign bottoms, or on foreign produce. We cannot, in the first instance, levy duties on the foreign trade, which passes the port of Calcutta to the settlements of Chinsurah,* Chandernagore, and Serampore, the river being free and open to them; but, by a sort of fiction, we treat those places as *ports beyond sea;* and, in order that the merchants frequenting them may not enjoy an exemption from the customs, we levy the import duty on all commodities coming from thence into our territory, and the export duty on goods passing from our territory to the foreign settlements. Their own consumption of articles imported from beyond sea, of course, escapes the tax.

At

---

* Chinsurah has now been ceded to us by the Dutch; but it is much to be regretted that these small settlements were restored at the peace. They are the source of inconvenience to us, without being the source of advantage to their possessors. The same may be said of the Portuguese settlements of Diu and Damaun, and even of Goa on the Malabar coast.

At a period not very remote, the customs were levied in almost every district in our western provinces, and goods proceeding from the Jumna to the Presidency, paid duties repeatedly in transitu, and were repeatedly detained for examination; but this system, which caused great embarrassment, delay, and expense to the merchant, has since been corrected. Town duties are still collected in the cities and principal towns as a means of taxing the consumption of those places; but as they are generally the resort of the more opulent, the tax is not, I think, justly liable to objections.

Under the circumstances in which British India is now placed, with her manufactures in a state of decay, and her trade to the mother country labouring under restrictions, it would not have been surprising if the customs had declined; but it will be satisfactory to find from the following abstract that this is not the case.

BENGAL CUSTOMS (ancient Territory).

	Receipts.	Charges.
1819-20	Ct. Rs. 42,77,870	Ct. Rs. 5,81,589
1820-21	44,48,417	5,89,846
1821-22	47,90,014	7,06,651

BENGAL CUSTOMS, including the " Ceded and Conquered Provinces."

	Receipts.	Charges.
1819-20	Ct. Rs. 73,82,537	Ct. Rs. 10,41,337
1820-21	82,48,810	10,77,567
1821-22	84,74,496	12,01,932

MADRAS

88

MADRAS CUSTOMS (ancient Territory).

	Receipts.		Charges.
1819-90 ...	Pagodas 4,54,282	...	Pagodas 1,27,145
1820-21	4,61,624		1,38,062
1821-22	5,66,101		1,74,395

The customs collected under the Madras Presidency, in the territory more recently acquired by us, appear also to have increased gradually, and they amounted in 1821-22 to the sum of Rupees 35,37,878. The customs at the port of Bombay appear to have been nearly stationary for several years.

In 1816-17 they amounted to......Rupees 9,82,001
And in 1821-22 to 10,28,624

There has, however, been a considerable augmentation of territory at Bombay, in consequence of the favourable termination of the late war with the Peishwa ; and the customs under this Presidency may now be stated as follow :—

Total collections in 1816-17, prior to the
late acquisitions .... Rupees 15,35,290
Collections in 1821-22....................34,33,708

It is scarcely necessary for me to mention that, in the observations which I have offered on the different branches of our revenue, I have had more especially in view the Presidency of Bengal, where 1 was myself employed ; but, in truth, this

is

is the great mine of our wealth. The revenues
of Fort St. George scarcely do more than defray
the charge of the civil and military establishments, the surplus at that Presidency, even during peace, having rarely exceeded the sum of
£300,000. At Bombay there has been always
a considerable deficit, which was supplied from
the surplus resources of Bengal. In 1816-17,
prior to the commencement of the late war,
it amounted to £1,042,056; but in consequence of our recent acquisitions, the deficit
has been reduced, in 1821-22, to the sum of
£754,154.

In addition to the branches of revenue already
enumerated, there are receipts at the different
Presidencies from various less important sources.
Peishcush, or tribute, from independent chiefs;
mint duties; post-office collections, &c. &c.;
but these did not appear to me to call for
explanation. I have, indeed, avoided, as far as
possible, all unnecessary details, which would
only have taxed unprofitably the attention of the
reader. My object has been to give a slight
sketch of the sources of our revenue; to examine, in a cursory manner, how far the different
branches of it are reconcileable with sound principles of policy; and to ascertain, from this examination, how far we may, with confidence, rely
upon their permanency, and upon their contain-

N   ing

ing within them the seeds of future improvement. The chief branch of our revenue still remains to be noticed ; and it is one which demands a distinct and a more deliberate consideration.

CHAPTER III.

LAND REVENUE OF INDIA.

I HAVE already observed that the land has, for ages, constituted the chief source of revenue in India, and I have endeavoured to explain the circumstances which have led to the adoption of this particular mode of taxation.

Prior to the administration of Lord Cornwallis, the land revenue had usually been let out to farm, sometimes for a single year, and sometimes for a period of five years; and occasionally whole districts were leased out to a single individual. In other instances, what is termed "*Khas*" management, was resorted to; that is, the European collector of a district, by means of the agency of native officers, collected the rents directly from the village communities, or individual occupants of the soil: and in both cases the rule seems to have been, to levy the utmost which the land would yield, without actually compelling the peasantry to desert their fields and homes.

This vicious system, which prevented the progress of cultivation, which had already impove-

rished

rished the country, and which threatened to reduce it to a state of irretrievable poverty and ruin,* soon attracted the notice of Lord Cornwallis; and after a long, patient, and able discussion, that upright statesman was convinced that considerations of justice, of humanity, and policy, all concurred to render a total change of plan absolutely necessary.

The revenue system, to which the just views of Lord Cornwallis disposed him to give a preference, involved questions of some difficulty. We were, at the time, imperfectly acquainted with the state of the country; our information with respect to the tenures under which the lands were held was incomplete; and we had not decided in whom the right of property in the land actually vested. The Zemindars (literally landholders) were generally supposed to be the proprietors,

---

* The following just description of the farming system is given in a letter from the Court of Directors, bearing date the 29th January 1813. " We observe that the revenue of a considerable proportion " of the lands, both in Etawah and Allighur, has been let in farm: " a system which, wherever it has obtained, experience has shewn to " be productive of fatal effects. It was this system which ruined " the Carnatic under the late Nabobs; and we fear that all the " modifications which may be applied to it under a British adminis- " tration, will fail in preventing its pernicious effects, &c. &c." See " Revenue Selections," page 76. I need not refer to the exaggerated description of the farming system given at the trial of Mr. Hastings, but it is notorious that it was productive of the most serious evils in Bengal, as well as in the Carnatic.

tors, partly from their Persian designation, and partly from their being found more generally in possession ; but it was maintained on the other hand, that these persons were mere officers of government, and that, according both to theory and usage, the sovereign, as lord paramount, possessed a right to a certain portion of the produce of every acre of land : others contended, that the Malicks, or village zemindars, were the rightful proprietors ; and others, again, that no right of property could be traced beyond the ryot (or husbandman), the heads of villages, or the village community, who cultivated the land in common.

It would be quite out of place were I to renew the discussion of a question, which is only incidentally connected with my subject, and which, as far as it regards the Bengal settlement, has been set at rest. I could not indeed pretend to throw any new light on what has been written on the landed tenures of India. The rights of the zemindars were contested by persons of high authority ; but Lord Cornwallis, who naturally revolted at the extravagant proposition of *the sovereign being the universal landlord,* at once cut the knot, by deciding, that if landholders did not exist, they ought to exist, and must be created ; and as a consequence of this determination the zemindars, whose connexion with the land was

more

more immediate and apparent, were recognized by our Government as the proprietors of the soil; a reservation being expressly made at the same time in favour of the rights of any other parties, who, by virtue of prescriptive usage or otherwise, might be able subsequently to establish an interest in the land.

That in assigning the lands, in the first instance, generally and indiscriminately to the zemindars, we may have overlooked the situation of other parties, having equal or superior claims, I am not prepared to deny ; nor can I deny that we may have attempted to reconcile things incompatible, by admitting a full right of property on the part of the zemindars, while we endeavoured at the same time to limit their demands for rent, and to preserve the right of occupancy to their ryots and under tenants. It must, moreover, be conceded, that Government, in the first instance, armed itself with more summary powers for collecting its *revenue,* than it was willing to entrust to the zemindar for collecting his *rent :* and the consequence was that the under tenants succeeding in some cases, by means of combination, in resisting for a time the demands of the landholders, several of the larger and more unmanageable estates were brought to sale, and passed away from the hereditary aristocracy of the country. They passed, no doubt, into the hands of

more

more prudent managers, and the subdivision of these principalities was favourable to the extension of agriculture; but still it is to be regretted that it should have taken place by any severe operation of our laws ; and, as frequently happens in such cases, the anxiety to correct one evil led to another in the opposite extreme. Regulation VII. of 1799, was enacted for the express purpose of relieving the zemindars : but it invested them with powers which are liable to be abused, and which have since been supposed to sanction a great degree of violence and oppression on their part.

Some minor objections may be urged against the recognition of the zemindarry right, before we had accurately ascertained and defined the rights of the inferior Talookdars, and others, who held an interest in the land under different tenures ; but it was considered necessary to take some decided step, and the Government proceeded upon the assumption, that all questions relating to the rights of these parties might safely be committed to the courts of justice. This would have been a safe and judicious course, if the laws had accurately defined rights, or if usage could have been safely referred to as authority, in a country where nothing had been stable, where no rights had been respected, and where, for a long series of years, the weak had been more or less at the mercy of the strong.

The

The next question to be decided was, whether the settlement to be made with the zemindars should be concluded for a term of years ? or whether the Government, limiting its demand upon the land, should declare the amount to be fixed in perpetuity ?*

I could not possibly, by any abridgment, do justice to the able discussion which took place between Lord Cornwallis and Mr. Shore (now Lord Teignmouth) on this important question ; and 1 shall, therefore, merely mention, that it was determined by his lordship, after mature deliberation, that the settlement should be declared permanent ; and that this determination was approved and confirmed by the authorities in England, in a letter from the Court of Directors, bearing date the 29th August 1792,† in which the principles of the settlement are reviewed with a spirit of liberality, and with a statesman-like comprehension, highly honourable to those from whom it proceeded.

Lord

* The plan of a permanent settlement was first urged upon the attention of Lord Cornwallis by Mr. Thomas Law, one of a family highly distinguished in this country in the Law and the Church. It was urged with characteristic ardour by one, who is an enthusiast in every thing which concerns the interests of humanity.

† This admirable letter is supposed to have been written under the immediate dictation of the late Lord Melville , and with the entire concurrence of the ministry of the day—Mr. Pitt—Lord Grenville, &c.

Lord Wellesley, actuated by similar views of an enlightened and benevolent policy, enacted certain regulations in the years 1803 and 1805, for the formation of a decennial settlement in the " Ceded and Conquered Provinces ;"* and in these regulations a formal pledge was given (subject to the approval and confirmation of the Court of Directors), that the settlement would be rendered permanent in all cases where the cultivation of the lands should have been sufficiently advanced, and the landholders should have punctually fulfilled their engagements with the Government throughout the term of the decennial lease.

The Honourable Court is understood to have recognized the promise made to the landholders of the " *Ceded* Provinces" by the regulations of 1803 ; but no such recognition appears to have been extended, otherwise than by implication, to the landholders of the " *Conquered* Provinces," although, the circumstances of the two cases being precisely similar, the spirit of the Honourable Court's instructions applied equally to both.†

Sir

* Regulations xxv, 1803, and ix, 1805.

† This question has been most ably examined by Mr. Edmonstone, in a late minute which unfortunately is not before the public. The Court of Directors, if they had disapproved of the promise made by the Supreme Government to the landholders of the Ceded Provinces in 1803, could scarcely have written as follows on the 28th August 1804 :—" As the permanent settlement for these extensive districts is " not to be carried into execution for ten years, from the commence-

o   " ment

Sir George Barlow and the late Lord Minto, impressed with a deep conviction of the great advantages which had resulted from the "permanent settlement," both to the Government and to the people, were solicitous to extend the benefit of the measure to the " ceded and conquered provinces," *even before the expiration of the decennial leases ;* and a board of commissioners was deputed in 1807, to those provinces, for the purpose of carrying the arrangement into immediate effect.

Upon grounds, however, which are fully detailed in a report* from the commissioners, bearing date the 13th April 1808, the expediency of postponing the measure, except in two particular instances, was strongly urged to the Government : it was accordingly suspended for the time ; and the country continuing from that period under temporary settlements, an encrease† of revenue has

" ment of the first triennial settlement, there will be full time, under
" the operation of that principle, and during the continuance of the
" respective periods of intermediate settlement, to ascertain their full
" value, and for enabling you *to conclude a permanent settlement* on
" such terms as shall be fair and equitable."—Mr. Edmonstone's excellent Minute should have put the question at rest for ever.

* See Report in " Revenue Selections," pages 6 to 44, by the commissioners, Messrs. Cox and Tucker. See also Mr. H. Colebrooke's Minute in reply to this Report, pages 44 *et seq.*

† This encrease is to be ascribed, in a great degree, to the able management of the late commissioners, Sir E. Colebrooke and Mr. Deane

has been obtained, abundantly sufficient to justify the delay which had been contended for by the commissioners in the first instance.

But the pledge of the Government to grant a " permanent settlement" *on the expiration of the decennial leases,* remained in full force ; and if in any one instance the two conditions of the pledge were complied with, (and it is matter of notoriety that they were complied with in very many instances,) the benefit of the measure could not be withheld without an absolute breach of faith. For the reasons which have caused it to be so long withheld, I must refer to the Honourable Court's

Deane, and to the indefatigable and successful exertions of some of the collectors under them, Mr. Trant, Mr. C. Lloyd, Mr. Ross, Mr. Christian, &c. The following comparison will shew the encrease of Revenue between 1808 and 1819 :—

	1807-8.	1818-19.	Encrease.
Land......... Sa. Rs.	2,18,78,040	3,14,92,570	96,14,530
Sayer	7,75,920	13,30,420	5,54,500
Customs	14,83,510	29,58,290	14,74,780
Total Sa. Rs...	2,41,37,470	3,57,81,280	1,16,43,810

Mr. Trant, by a course of laborious exertion, increased the revenue of one district in the sum of £100,000 per annum, *viz.*

Bareilly: amount of first triennial settlement in 1803, Rs. 22,97,588
Mr. Trant's settlement in 1809-10.........................31,65,495

Encrease... Rupees 8,67,907

Court's letter to Bengal, of the 16th March*
1813, and other official correspondence on the
subject. It has been stated, that it would be inconvenient to sanction two different kinds of
settlement, permanent in one place, and temporary in another; but this objection is not entitled
to the slightest weight, even if considerations of
expediency could be admitted to supersede the
obligations of justice. Mokurrery and Istimrary
grants (perpetual grants at a fixed assessment),
were made not unfrequently by our Mahomedan
predecessors; and the people throughout our provinces were familiarized and attached to them,
long before they had before their eyes the " permanent settlement" concluded by Lord Cornwallis in the Bengal districts. If one single
landholder had then complied with our conditions, *his* claim ought to have been admitted,
and we could have no plea for withholding the
boon, on the ground that his neighbours had not
performed *their* engagements. By conceding *his*
right, we should not only have done an act of
justice, but we should have encouraged others to
follow his salutary example.

It is of importance to all governments that they
should preserve faith with their subjects; but
situated as we are in India, our dominion resting
in a great degree upon *moral influences*, it is of
peculiar

† See " Revenue Selections," pages 136 *et seq.*

peculiar importance that we should command the confidence and esteem of the people. By granting fixed tenures, and limiting the public demand upon the land, we give the landholders an interest in the stability of our Government. This is a great point gained in any part of our territory ; but it is more especially desirable and essential to our security, that such an interest should be excited in our favour in our western provinces, where we have an open frontier accessible to our most formidable enemies, and where we have a brave and warlike population, ready at all times to exchange the ploughshare for the sword.* The *peasantry* of Rohilkund in 1794, boldly encountered,

* See Secret Letter from Bengal—" Revenue Selections," page 134, para. 17. " It is under circumstances, such as we have just stated, " that we are commanded to announce to the great body of the " people, that the permanency of the Jumma no longer exists. The " assurances given to the landholders in the years 1803 and 1805, and " which for the reasons already stated, we consider to be in full " force and effect, may, in some degree, alleviate the disappointment " which must be experienced from the operation of the present " orders. Still it is impossible to judge, à priori, of the effects with " which that disappointment may be attended. It is a feeling which " is nearly allied to discontent; and when these impressions are felt " in any considerable degree, resistance to public authority is always " to be apprehended. The people have furnished on affairs of com- " paratively small and trivial interest, examples of a disposition to " assist their wishes by tumult and outrage. A more powerful in- " citement to seek redress by combination and violence, cannot be " given in any country, and cannot extend to a larger and more " powerful class of the community than injustice supposed to be " done to the great body of landed proprietors."

tered, and nearly defeated, a large army of regulars, under the personal command of a gallant and experienced officer.*

The public authorities in Bengal, with scarcely an exception, have all concurred in the propriety of redeeming our pledge to the landholders of the " Ceded and Conquered Provinces," both on grounds of justice and of policy. We have had the country under our management for twenty years, and have become acquainted with its situation and resources ; those resources have been gradually developed and improved ; and we have been enabled, in consequence, to add above a million sterling to our annual revenue ; and we have had, at the same time, an opportunity of acquiring better information with respect to the nature of the tenures and other circumstances, which it was necessary to ascertain, in order that we might not compromise the rights of different parties, whose interests might be affected by the settlement.

The Court of Directors do not, I believe, profess to be solicitous to augment the ample revenue which is, at present, derived from the " Ceded and Conquered Provinces ;" and few persons will now be found so visionary as to fancy that perfect equality in the assessment, even if it were practicable in the first instance, and absolutely

essential

* Sir Robert Abercrombie, Commander-in-Chief in India.

essential at any time, could long be preserved in a country, where changes in the course of agriculture and of commerce, must necessarily occasion variations in the value of agricultural productions. In a particular estate, the introduction of the cultivation of Indigo alone, may double the value of the produce; while in a neighbouring zemindarry, originally of equal value, some unfavourable change may take place to reduce its natural resources.

Still, there are persons who, witnessing the flourishing condition of the Bengal provinces, and knowing that the rents and income of the Zemindars have, in many instances, been immoderately encreased, seem disposed to impute to Lord Cornwallis an improvident sacrifice of the public revenue. *The inference is as gratuitous. as the imputation is unjust.* The prosperity of the country and the growing opulence of the zemindars, are *the happy effects* of the " permanent settlement."

Those effects would probably never have been produced, if the settlement had never been made. Secure to man the produce of his industry, and he will be industrious. Provide for the security of his property, and it will be embarked in works of public utility, advantageous to the individual, and beneficial to the community at large. But if the deadly hand of the tax-gatherer perpetually

ually hover over the land and threaten to grasp that which is not yet called into existence, its benumbing influence must be fatal, and the fruits of the earth will be stifled in the very germ.

Lord Cornwallis was the benefactor* of British India, and the " permanent settlement" is, perhaps, " the noblest monument of a just and " liberal policy, which was ever erected in a " conquered country." But we must not look to this great measure as the sole and exclusive source of the prosperity of our Bengal provinces. Lord Cornwallis did not stop here ; he introduced sound principles, and a just system of revenue administration.

1st. He separated the revenue and judicial authorities, and thus put an end to that monopoly of power, which not only leads to abuse, but which tends at the same time to secure to it impunity.

2dly. He established independent courts, to whose

---

* Lord Cornwallis did almost as much for British India as General Washington for America; and, I fancy, strong points of resemblance between these eminent personages : they possessed alike dignity of character united with simplicity of manners and habits ; firmness of purpose ; undeviating rectitude; disinterestedness; prudence; moderation ; patriotism. The difference between them may be referred to the circumstances of their birth. Had those circumstances been reversed, Lord Cornwallis would probably have been the leader of a republican army, and General Washington the pride of the British peerage and a pillar of the throne.

whose jurisdiction both the government and its officers were made amenable for all official acts.

3dly. He established a code of regulations, which supplied a rule of conduct to the public officers ; which assured personal freedom and protection to our native subjects ; which explained in every case the reason for the enactment ; which softened and corrected the barbarisms* of the Mahomedan law ; and which, however immature and imperfect, must be regarded as a great advance in the difficult science of legislation from a state approaching to anarchy, and the absence of all law.

Lastly, he assigned to the officers of government

* For example. The punishment of mutilation was abolished, and the heir of the slain was deprived of the right of making his election between " *Deeut*" and " *Kissaas*"—(the price of blood, or retaliation). The government of India is often reproached for having subverted the native institutions ; but those who prefer the charge, have seldom been at the pains to specify the institutions which have been displaced, or superseded. Lord Cornwallis, it is true, abolished the office of hereditary canoongo (an office for recording grants, titles, usages, boundary lines, revenue accounts, &c.) ; and this was, I think, a mistake. The office had become corrupt, and had fallen into disrepute ; but it would have been more prudent if we had endeavoured to reform its abuses, instead of sweeping it away altogether. The registry, which was established as a substitute for it, was found quite inefficient ; and existed, indeed, only in the regulations. My colleague (Mr. Cox), and myself proposed the continuance of the office in the western provinces ; and, at a subsequent period, its re-establishment in Bengal, in a modified shape. It has since been revived.

P

ment fair and liberal allowances, which placed them above temptation ; which took away every plea and excuse for peculation ; and which, by rendering the service independent and respectable, raised its character, inspired it with a higher tone of feeling, and secured our native subjects, as far as this can be done by such means, against official malversation.

These are among the solid benefits conferred by Lord Cornwallis on the people of Bengal. It is not attempted to conceal that the " permanent settlement " may have been open to objections. To the natives of India, within whose narrow horizon every thing had hitherto announced uncertainty, and an evanescent existence, leases for a term of twenty or twenty-one years, or for the lives of the incumbents, would, probably, have been received with nearly the same sentiments as a perpetuity ; and such leases as preparatory to a permanent settlement would, no doubt, have furnished an opportunity for correcting *gross* inequalities in the assessment. It might also, perhaps, have been practicable to secure the proprietors of the unwieldy zemindarries against the consequences of that improvidence and dissipation, which their early education and acquired habits were likely to produce ; and if the antient families could have been pre-

served

served in their possessions* by any safe and un-objectionable means, the credit of the British Government would certainly have been raised in the eyes of the people. But with all its imperfections, real or imputed, the " permanent settlement," as the source of *genuine good,* stands unrivalled among all the measures of our administration in India. By limiting the demand of the exchequer, the residuary produce of industry became a property, and the labour of the country was stimulated into active employment. A wilderness, as if by magic, was converted into a garden ;† capital was created ; the surplus produce

* The zemindarry of Burdwan, paying an annual revenue to government of £400,000, remains entire, I believe, to the present day. The zemindarries next in extent, and equal at least in antiquity (those of Rajeshahy and Nuddeah), have both, I fear, been broken down, and sold ; but certainly not as a consequence of *over-assessment.* Some of the estates of more moderate extent (such as that of Tikarry in Bahar), which were of little value before the assessment was fixed, yield at present princely incomes to their proprietors ; and we ought to rejoice at this, instead of regretting the supposed sacrifice of revenue. There is reason, perhaps, for regret, that the estates which have been sold, had not been sequestrated for a time, by which means they might have been preserved to the ancient proprietors.

† The change in the state of our Bengal provinces within the last thirty years, is so much matter of notoriety, that it would be quite superfluous to adduce written evidence of the extraordinary improvement which has taken place. Many of us have witnessed it with our own eyes. Nor is it necessary for me to insist that the revenue is now collected with ease and with scarcely the fraction of a balance ; whereas, heretofore, the collections were made with great severity,

and

duce of the soil was preserved ; and the abundance of one province, or of one season, supplied the deficiencies of another. Famine, that scourge of a numerous population, has been averted, as far as it can be averted by human means ; and during a period of thirty-five years, in which unfavourable seasons and deficient harvests have certainly been experienced, Bengal has not only enjoyed plenty at home, but has assisted largely in supplying the wants of other countries.

I now come to the consideration of a measure of a totally different complexion.

While the plan of a permanent settlement was popular in England, steps had been taken to extend its benefits to the territory under the government of Fort St. George, and considerable progress had been made in introducing it into the districts under that Presidency ; but at a subsequent period, an entire change of sentiment appears unfortunately to have taken place, both in the Court of Directors and at the Board of Control ;* and, instead of prosecuting to a conclusion

and the balances at the end of every year were considerable. Moreover, periodical settlements were the never-failing source of *periodical corruption and abuse.*

* I might also add in Parliament, if the 5th Report of a Committee of the House of Commons, which was drawn up by two individuals, highly respectable and estimable, but altogether unconnected with that Body, can be supposed to have expressed the sense of Parliament.

sion the undertaking which had been commenced, there was a disposition to trace back our steps, to undo what had been done, and even to purchase upon account of government, those estates in which the settlement had been actually concluded in perpetuity.

I am unwilling to believe that this change had any connection with a design or wish to encrease the public revenue; and if any such expectation were cherished, it has certainly been disappointed. Novel doctrines were, in fact, brought forward, which impeached the principle of the settlement; and a system of revenue administration was recommended to a preference, on various grounds; but chiefly on an assumption that it harmonized better with the habits and dispositions of our native subjects, and was more in accordance with the usages and institutions of the country.

This plan of management, which is now familiarly known as the " *Ryotwar* system," found an able, intelligent, and zealous advocate in Sir Thomas Munro, the present governor of Fort St. George; and in delineating its character, I propose, as far as possible, to use his own words, while, in offering my own free comments upon the merits of the system, 1 hope not to deviate from the respect which is due to such high authority.

Sir T. Munro advances the following singular
pro-

proposition; and, startling as the dictum* may appear, it was a necessary preliminary to clear the ground for the structure intended to be erected.

" But nothing can be plainer than that *private* " *landed property has never existed in India,* " excepting on the Malabar coast; and that, " therefore, in all other districts, the share of " the produce which ought to constitute the rent " to Government, must be determined rather by " opinion than by experience."† Again : " In " the Ceded Districts and throughout the Dec- " can, the Ryot has little or no property in land ; " he has no possessory right : he does not even " claim it; he is so far from asserting either a " proprietory or possessory right, that he is " always ready to relinquish his land and take " some other which he supposes is lighter as- " sessed. All land is supposed to revert to Go- " vernment at the end of every year, to be dis-
" tributed

---

* I find this dictum quoted, and most satisfactorily controverted, by a writer for whom I have the greatest respect. See History of the South of India, by Col. M. Wilks, vol. 1, pages 105 *et seq.* The whole of Chapter 5, containing a dissertation on the Landed Property of India, claims particular attention. It did not occur to me to look into this valuable treatise, until I had finished these pages; but I have had the satisfaction to find my opinion, with respect to the existence of private property in land in India, completely confirmed.

† See " Revenue Selections," pages 95 and 102.

" tributed as it may think proper ; and land is
" accordingly sometimes taken from one ryot
" and given to another, who is willing to pay a
" higher rent. If this power is exercised with
" caution, it is not from the fear of violating
" any possessory right, but of losing revenue ;
" for the assessment is generally so high, that if
" the ryot is dispossessed, the same rent can
" seldom be got from a new one."*

The state of things here announced can scarcely
be said to exist, even in the first stage of the
human race. The savage has a notion of property, and retains possession of the hunting
ground which he first occupied, defending it *as
his own,* until he is ejected from it by a stronger
arm.

I will not appeal to the Altumga and other
royal grants of the Mahomedan rulers, which are
every where to be met with, nor to the Birmooter
and other religious grants of the Hindoos, which are
to be found in every part of the country ; because
these, as well as the " Enam" or free grants, may
be considered as *alienations* of the royal domain,
which do not come within the precise terms of
the proposition ; but if I were called upon to
point out the country where landed property is
most highly appreciated and cherished, where
landed

* See " Revenue Selections." Pages 95 and 102.

landed possessions are most tenaciously retained, and where the land makes up the sum and essence of all which the individual can properly call *his own*, I should point to *India*. I do not mean to aver that the people enjoy English freeholds, protected by courts of justice of a structure highly artificial, and fenced round by laws and elaborate forms which almost preclude the conveyance of a title; but I do contend that land was held as private property in India; and that it was respected as such, although often the object of extortion and violence, by the ruling power.*

When a proposition is enunciated, apparently at variance with all our experience and with the ordinary course of human affairs, we may fairly require

---

* It is impossible to read the description of " *Meeràs*" and " *Wuttun*" in the correspondence of the public officers at Madras, and in Mr. Elphinstone's report on the Marhatta territories, without being satisfied that these tenures constituted *complete hereditary property*. The sovereign himself was compelled sometimes to purchase land held under these tenures, at very high prices; and what has effaced in some places every trace of private property in land? Nothing but *over-assessment*, which has compelled the people to abandon their possessions. Some of the collectors observe, that " light *assessment creates private property in land*." True: just as heavy assessment destroys it. " *Meeràs*" is an Arabic word, signifying inheritance, which must have been introduced by the Mahomedans; so that we see these despotic conquerors acknowledging a right, which an enlightened British government seems disposed now to question. Numerous decisions might be cited, recognizing a right of property in the land to vest in the Meerassydars of the Carnatic.

require that it be established by precise and satisfactory evidence; but in this instance we have
to deal with a *negative* proposition, which can be
met and refuted only by establishing the affirma-
tive: still the party denying generally, has no
right to shelter himself in a defensive position, if
a single instance can be cited which contra-
dicts the negative averment. It might safely
have been affirmed a century ago, that the elec-
tric fluid could not be brought down from the
clouds by means of a string, or that flame could
not be made to issue out of water; but after the
exhibition of a single experiment in proof of these
facts, we should not be entitled to insist further
in denying them.*

I shall content myself, therefore, with adducing
a single instance, for the purpose of shewing that
the people of Bengal, at least, not only possessed
land, but manfully resisted any attempt to usurp
or alienate it on the part of the sovereign. The
document† which is given in a note below, contains

---

* Sir T. Munro admits an exception from his proposition on the
coast of Malabar; but if the sphere of his observation had been
extended, the exception would, I think, have been found to be
the rule. Sir T. M. had the merit of giving to landed property in
Canara, a real value, by lowering the oppressive rates of assessment
established by Hyder Ali and Tippoo Sultan in that province, and
Malabar.

† Inscription on a rock at Tàràchandi, near Sahasram, in South
Bahar, from a fac simile, taken by the learned Dr. Buchanan Hamil-

Q   ton,

tains the protest of a Hindoo landholder against
grant made by the rajah, or sovereign of
Canouge, in favour of certain priests, to the prejudice of the rights of the party : it is dated in
1229 Sanvat, or 1173 of the Christian æra; and
it is curious to observe a Hindoo boldly remon-
strating against the act of his liege lord, at a
time when our Saxon ancestors were suffering
grievous oppressions from their Norman conquerors, without daring to resist their violence
and usurpations.

The

ton, and translated by the distinguished Oriental scholar, Mr. H. Colebrooke. " *Pràtàpa dhavala*, wholly divine (dèva), possessor of hap-
" pily-risen and celebrated glory, addresses his own race. In these
" villages contiguous to *Callahaudi*, that contemptible ill-copper
" (grant) which has been obtained by fraud and bribery from the
" slaves of the Sovereign of Gódhinagara, by priests sprung from
" *Sa-valuhala ;* there is no ground of faith to be put therein by the
" people around. Not a bit of land, so much as a needle's point
" might pierce, is theirs."
" Sanvat 1229 (A. D. 1173) *Iyeshta vadi* 3d Wednesday. The
" feet of the sovereign of *Jápela*, the great chieftain, the fortunate
" *Pràtàpa Dhavala dèva*, declares the truth to his sons, grandsons,
" and other descendants sprung of his race. This ill-copper (grant)
" of the villages of *Callahaudi* and *Bidaypita*, obtained by fraud and
" bribery from the slaves of the fortunate *Vijaya Chandra*, the king
" sovereign of *Canyacabja*, by plundering folks: no faith is to be
" placed therein. Those priests are every way libertines. Not so
" much land as might be pierced by a needle's point, is theirs. Know-
" ing this, you will take the share of produce and other dues ; or——"
" Signature · of the great Rajaputrà (king's son), the fortunate
" Satrughira."

The protest shews in a very striking manner the strong feeling which existed at a remote period with regard to landed property, and the jealousy with which any encroachment was viewed by the landholder. In the present case, the right of the prince to make grants for religious purposes, does not seem to be denied ; but it is practically resisted on the ground that the grant was fraudulently obtained, or was an imposition ; and the protest, by recording the transaction, appears to have been intended to keep the alienation in view, that the heirs and descendants of the landholder might reassert and resume their rights, whenever a favourable opportunity should occur.

It may be urged, that this sturdy rajepoot was some powerful feudatory, who was in a condition to defy his liege lord ; some duke of Burgundy resisting a king of France; but the pompous titles which he assumes are not sufficient to warrant such a conclusion.

The mountain of " *Rotas*," situated at no great distance from Sahàsram (Sasseram), is certainly a strong natural fortification, where a refractory chief might, no doubt, have bade defiance to his sovereign ; but Sahàsram is itself situated in an open country ; and the proud rajepoot who was strong enough to dispute the encroachments of his liege, would have been much more likely

to

to make his appeal to the sword than to the pen.

This single instance must be admitted as evidence of the *understanding of the people* upon the question of property in land ; but let us ascend to the source, in order to determine whether the popular feeling is in unison with the law.

I own myself incompetent to the task of disentangling a text of Hindoo law* from the subtilties of commentators, so as to reduce it to a simple elementary proposition ; but on this occasion I have fortunately the authority and assistance of the eminent orientalist, to whom we are indebted for the translation of the digest of that law.

The Mimànsà, which is the subject of a dissertation by Mr. Colebrooke, is a work of great authority among the Hindoos, professedly treating upon the rules of interpretation, and principles of construction, applicable to the precepts of the *Vèda*, and maxims of law, religious and civil. The question concerning property in the soil in India, is discussed in the sixth lecture of that work, and the following quotation is calculated to shew the view

* See " Digest of Hindoo Law," vol. ii, pages 74 and 75, in which the distinction between the property of the subject and the rights of the sovereign, is drawn; but all which can be safely affirmed is, that property, or ownership, vests in the occupant of the soil, " founded on the reason of the law and on settled usage ;" but that it is subject to qualifications and restrictions in favour of the sovereign rights.

view taken of this important question by the author.

" At certain sacrifices, such as that which is
" called Visivajit, the votary for whose benefit the
" religious ceremony is performed, is enjoined to
" bestow all his property on the officiating priests.
" It is asked whether a paramount sovereign
" shall give all the land, including pasture
" ground, highways, and the site of lakes and
" ponds? — an universal monarch the whole
" earth? — and a subordinate prince the entire
" province over which he rules? To that ques-
" tion the answer is, the *monarch has not pro-*
" *perty in the earth, nor the subordinate sovereign*
" *in the land.* By conquest the kingly power is
" obtained, and property in the house and field
" that belonged to the enemy. The maxim of
" the law, that the king is the lord of all, sacer-
" dotal wealth excepted, concerns his authority
" for correction of the wicked, and protection of
" the good ; his kingly power is for the protec-
" tion of the realm, and extirpation of wrong,
" and for that cause he receives taxes (*cara*) from
" husbandmen, and levies fines from offenders.
" *But a right of property is not thereby vested in*
" *him ;* else he would have property in house
" and land appertaining to the subjects abiding
" in his dominions. ' It belongs,' says Jaimini,
" ' to all alike.' Therefore, although a gift of a
                                        " piece

118

" piece of ground, an individual's property, does
" take place, the whole land cannot be given by
" a monarch, nor a province by a subordinate
" prince ; but house and field, acquired by pur-
" chase, and similar means, are liable to gift."
It is not necessary for me to cite the various
authorities which are referred to, in support of the
text ; nor shall I look further for the proof of that
which is found to exist, in a degree more or less
perfect, under the most despotic and barbarous
governments.* The Hindoos are a people whose
law

* In addition to other authorities, I have in my possession copy
of a report by Major James Tod, on the state of landed property
in Meywar, a pure Hindoo district, little affected in its internal
arrangements by Mahomedan intrusion. Major Tod has not only
had the benefit of much practical experience, but he has made Hindoo literature and history the particular object of his study; and
his opinion is decidedly in favour of the existence of private property in land in India. The historian of British India considers the
right of property to vest in the sovereign. See vol 1, pages 179,
et seq.: but Mr. Mill makes, at the same time, certain admissions
in favour of the ryot. " By practice the possession of the ryot be-
" came, in this manner, a permanent possession; a possession from
" which he was not removed except when he failed to pay his
" assessment, or rent ; a possession which he could sell during his
" life, or leave by inheritance, when he died. As far as rights can
" be established by prescription, these rights came undoubtedly to be
" established in the case of the ryots in India. And to take them
" away is one of the most flagrant violations of property which it is
" possible to commit," If the rights of *occupancy*—of *sale*—and of
bequest (to which we may add that of *mortgage*) be admitted, we go
far to establish *ownership*, and the only further question in this case
would be, whether the *object* of this ownership be a thing of any
value.

law inculcates submission to their princes and
their priests; but they are a civilized people, and
it is difficult to believe that they can, at any
period

value. Despotic power may render the property in land of no value
—it may efface all rights—and it may set up pretensions of its own
in the place of those which it has obliterated; but this is plain usur-
pation. To say that the sovereign is universal owner of the soil, is
to say neither more nor less than that power may, or can, destroy all
rights. Of the right, however, (under sufferance of the sovereign,
if it must be so) to occupy—to sell—to mortgage—and to bequeathe
land, we have incontestible evidence in numberless authentic deeds,
which have been produced by parties, who are not merely *ryots*.
The just observations of Mr. Mill, applied to the *ryot*, may, therefore, with equal justice be applied to these parties; but without undertaking to advocate the claims of any particular class of landholders, I contend that the pretensions of the sovereign to universal
ownership, can be admitted only upon the assumption of an unmiti-
gated despotism, which recognizes no rights in opposition to its un-
controlled will. I am aware that the Hindoo law seems to require
the sanction of the sovereign to all transfers of landed property;
but this may be explained in two ways. 1st. The sovereign having an
interest in the land from which he draws *revenue*, would naturally
require all deeds of sale or mortgage to be formally registered, in order
to preserve regularity, and in order, perhaps, to give security to the
title of the purchaser. This is done in Scotland universally, at the
present day, and for the reason suggested. 2dly. The sovereign, on
failure of natural heirs, being the universal heir of his subjects, had
a reversionary interest in the land; and his concurrence was required
as an heir of entail, just as the concurrence of the co-sharers, sons,
and others, holding an immediate or reversionary interest in the
estate, appears to have been required by the Hindoo law. Both
Hindoos and Mahomedans rigidly insisted upon the registry of all
transfers of land; and a fee of two per cent. (sud-doee) was, I believe, levied by the Canoongos of Bengal, on the transfer even of
Lakheràje land, or land held exempt from taxation.

period of their history, have renounced, in favour of kingly power, the idea of private property, and those feelings which are common to the whole human race.

I am far from undertaking to decide between the claims of different descriptions of landholders in India; and it would be unsafe to attach any particular weight to the designations which they respectively bear. The meaning of the term "*zemindar*" is, no doubt, landholder; that of "*malick*," proprietor; that of "*meerassydar*," heritor. But the application of these and other designations, is different in different places—for example : in Bengal Proper, the zemindar is the principal landholder, and the talookdar the dependent, or tenant ; whereas, in our western provinces, the case is reversed, and the talookdar is the principal, and the village zemindar the inferior landholder, or yeoman.

Sir T. Munro having assumed that the government was lord paramount of the soil, and as such free to make those arrangements which might be most conducive to the public interests, proceeded, with the sanction of the Madras Government, to form the settlement of the country entrusted to his charge, upon the following plan and principles.

" 1st. The settlement shall be ryotwarry."

" 2d. The amount of the settlement shall
" encrease

" encrease and decrease annually, according to
" the extent of the land in cultivation."

" 3d. A reduction of twenty-five per cent on
" all land shall be made in the survey rate of
" assessment."

" 4th. An additional reduction in the assess-
" ment of eight per cent., or thirty-three per cent.
" in all, shall be allowed on all lands watered by
" wells, or by water raised by machinery from
" rivers and nullahs, provided the cultivators keep
" the wells or embankments (dirroas) in repair
" at their own expense. A similar reduction
" shall be allowed on the lands watered by small
" tanks, whenever the cultivators agree to bear
" the expense of repairs."

" 5th. Every ryot shall be at liberty, at the end
" of every year, either to throw up a part of his
" land, or to occupy more, according to his cir-
" cumstances; but whether he throw up or oc-
" cupy, shall not be permitted to *select;* but
" shall take or reject proportional shares of the
" good and bad together."

" 6th. Every ryot, as long as he pays the rent
" of his land, shall be considered as the complete
" owner of the soil, and shall be at liberty to let
" it to a tenant without any hesitation as to rent,
" and to sell it as he pleases."

" 7th. No remission shall be made on ordinary
" occasions for bad crops or other accidents.

R   " Should

" Should failures occur, which cannot be made
" good from the property or land of the defaul-
" ters, *the village in which they happen shall be*
" *liable for them, to the extent of ten per cent. addi-*
" *tional on the rent of the remaining ryots ; but no*
" *farther.*"

" 8th. All unoccupied land shall remain in the
" hands of Government, and the rent of whatever
" part of it may be hereafter cultivated, shall be
" added to the public revenue."

" 9th. All taxes on houses, shops, and profes-
" sions ; all duties, licences, &c.—shall belong
" exclusively to Government. The ryot on whose
" lands houses or shops may be built, shall not
" be entitled to receive a higher rent from them
" than the equivalent of the survey rent of the
" ground which they occupy."

" 10th. The repairs of all tanks, which are not
" rendered private property by an extra remis-
" sion, or *duswundum-enam,* shall be made at the
" expense of Government."

" 11th. Tuckavy (*i. e.* advances to the culti-
" vators) shall be gradually discontinued."

" 12th. Potails, curnums, and all other vil-
" lage servants, shall remain, as hertofore, under
" the collector."

" 13th. Private creditors who may distrain the
" property of ryots, shall discharge the rent
" which may be due from such ryots to Govern-
" ment ;

" ment ; and shall give security for it before they
" begin to distrain."*

It would not be difficult to predicate what a
philosopher in his closet would think of a system,
which levels every thing in a country between the
sovereign and the labouring peasant ; but when
plans come recommended from high authority, on
the ground of experience, we are bound to pause
ere we admit the deductions of theory. Still, we
must not so far defer to authority as to receive,
without examination, propositions which seem to
run counter to our reason ; and I propose, therefore, to canvas those parts of the plan, which a
person of common understanding may be supposed
capable of appreciating.

The basis of Sir T. Munro's settlement is *an
actual survey of the land.* Native officers, deno-
minated "gomashtahs," were deputed into the
country " in parties of six, but afterwards of ten,"
for the purpose of measuring every field.† " Head
surveyors, or inspectors," were afterwards employed, to examine the measurement of the surveyors, or gomashtahs. " The surveyors were
" followed by assessors, two of whom were
" allotted

* See Report of Sir T. Munro in " Revenue Selections," pages
98 and 99.

† See Sir T. Munro's detailed instructions to the surveyors and
assessors, pages 121 to 137, " Revenue Selections."

" allotted for the assessment of the land mea-
" sured by each party of ten surveyors. The
" assessor, on arriving in a village, went over the
" land with the potail, curnum, and ryots, and
" arranged it in different classes according to its
" quality. In all villages, the land, both wet
" and dry, had, from ancient custom, been divi-
" ded into first, second, and third sorts, agreeably
" to their supposed respective produce; but these
" divisions not being sufficiently minute for a
" permanent settlement, the classes of wet land in
" a village were often encreased to five or six, and
" those of dry to eight or ten."*

But as these assessors could not be entirely depended upon, it was thought advisable, for the
purpose of preserving uniformity and of checking
abuses, to appoint five "head assessors," selected
from the most intelligent of the ordinary assessors.
Each head assessor had four ordinary ones under
him; his business was to review their classifica-
tion and assessment, and to correct them when
wrong.

After this preparatory process, the settlement
is

* See Sir T. Munro's Letter of the 26th July 1807—" Revenue
Selections," pages 116 et seq. These surveys were attended with an
enormous expense. That of the " Ceded Districts "· cost 83,000
pagodas (or above £33,000); and, as the revenue of those districts
was only 16,00,000 pagodas, the charge exceeded five per cent.
See page 121.

is concluded with the ryots, sometimes by the
European collector, but more generally by his
native officers; for Sir T. Munro observes,*
" The most experienced collector could hardly
" make the settlement of ten villages in a whole
" year, and after all it would most likely be
" done very indifferently."† And, that experienced officer remarks in another place, " Even
" where the ryots neglect to bring the grievance
" forward

---

* See Sir T. Munro's Letter of the 30th November 1806—" Revenue Selections," page 94.

† If this be the utmost which an *experienced* collector can accomplish, what is to be expected from an *inexperienced* collector, as
described by Mr. Thackery, one of the advocates of the " Ryotwar
System ?" He observes, " Over-zealous, but honourable young men,
" might plunder the country more completely, perhaps, than a Mar-
" hatta army could have done." Now, this system, embracing as it
does multitudinous details, requires a greater number of collectors
than any other ; or (what is worse) a greater number of native officers.
—See, also, Mr. Thackery's opinion of *Surveys*—" Revenue Selections," page 859. " If, indeed, the survey had been equal at first,
" and could continue so, no loss would result from this freedom (*i. e.*
" liberty to throw up over-assessed lands), because the rent being
" every where exactly proportioned to the value of the land, the
" ryot, wherever he went, and whatever extent of land he occupied,
" would have to pay the proportionate rent. But, no survey rate
" can be so nicely adjusted at first; and, if it could, would soon
" change. The value and rent of land fluctuates like the value of
" any thing else. But, even at first, we cannot so nicely appraise
" earth; and, if we could, ten thousand mistakes must find their way
" into a survey. Frauds cannot be prevented, and erroneous principles
" are frequently adopted." And yet this is to be the foundation of
the Ryotwar Settlement !

" forward immediately, they hardly ever omit to
" state it when assembled for the settlement of
" the ensuing year; and the tehsildar, knowing
" that gross negligence or partiality will be at-
" tended with the loss of his place, seldom ven-
" tures to make an unfair settlement. There
" are, however, cases in which he does so, either
" from ignorance or corrupt motives; but where
" the collector is vigilant, they are not frequent.
" There is, indeed, no possibility of preventing
" them altogether; for the collector, when he
" makes the settlement in person, may be de-
" ceived occasionally by the servants of his own
" cutcherry, who may be dishonest as well as the
" tehsildar. The business of a collector is not
" properly so much to labour through all the
" details of the settlement, as to make those do
" it who can do it best. The potails and cur-
" nums of villages, are the persons most capable
" of making the settlements correctly; but they
" cannot be trusted, because they are cultivators
" themselves, and have always friends and ene-
" mies among the ryots. It, therefore, becomes
" necessary to employ a tehsildar,* who, *not*
" *being*

* See Sir T. Munro's Letter of the 30th November 1806—" Revenue Collections," page 93.
Then read Mr. Ravenshaw's character of a Tehsildar—" Revenue
Selections," page 113, para. 12. " Hence arises that want of energy,
" that deplorable negligence, shameful ignorance, and, in some cases,
corruption;

" being a native of the district, is not so liable to
" be influenced by partialities."

The settlement appears to be made by assembling the ryots, or cultivators, early in the year ;
and *" when a country has been surveyed,** the
" indi-

" corruption; for which the generality of the tehsildars and other
" native servants are so remarkable in this soubah (Arcot). I have
" met with very few who know any other village than their cusba,
" who know any thing of the resources of their districts, or who can
" give a satisfactory answer to any question relative thereto."
" Para. 16. " Such is the present indolence as well as ignorance
" of the generality of tehsildars, that I have little hope of their exe-
" cuting the orders sent them with any degree of vigour, unless they
" are stimulated thereto by your presence in the talooks."
Next, read Sir T. Munro's own description of his Revenue Servants, in vol. ii. of Judicial Selections, page 231, Report 10th April
1806, para. 56. " As there is a general combination down to the
" lowest village servant against the collectors, it is not easy for him
" to learn what is going on; and when he has made the discovery, he
" perhaps only removes one set of servants, to make way for another
" equally corrupt: and hence, in order to prevent their falling
" into similar practices, he is forced to act rather as a spy, than in the
" superintendance of the province committed to his charge. Of
" about a hundred principal division and district servants who have
" acted under me during the last seven years, there have not been
" more than five or six against whom peculation to a greater or
" smaller extent has not been proved."
* The following is the opinion of the Supreme Government with
respect to surveys :—See Letter of the 14th December 1811—
" Revenue Selections," pages 174 and 175. " In treating of the
" advantages which may be derived from actual surveys, your Honour-
" able Court observe, that ' in the management of the Conquered
" and Ceded Territories which have been annexed to the two subor-
" dinate Presidencies, this course has been successfully pursued,'
" &c.

" individual supersedes both the village and dis-
" trict settlement, because it is then no longer
" necessary to waste time in endeavouring to
" persuade the cultivators to accede to the as-
" sessment. The rent of every field being fixed,
" each cultivator takes, or rejects, what he
" pleases, and the rents of all the fields occupied
" in the course of the year in any one village,
" form what is called the settlement of that vil-
" lage."* But where the lands have not been
sur-

" &c. Possessing only general knowledge of the measures adopted
" with a view to the adjustment of the assessment in the territories
" dependent on the Presidencies of Fort St. George and Bombay,
" and of the effect of those measures, we are necessarily precluded
" from offering any opinion upon the expediency of the surveys made
" in those parts of the British dominions; but the experience ob-
" tained on the subject in Bengal, would by no means warrant us in
" recommending that a similar course should be observed in the terri-
" tories dependent on this.Presidency. In former times, recourse
" was not unfrequently had to this expedient; but the chicanery and
" corruption practised by the large body of native officers necessarily
" employed in the performance of that duty, the exactions and injus-
" tice to which the zemindars were consequently exposed, and the
" heavy expense with which all such surveys were attended, gradually
" induced succeeding governments to abandon the plan of fixing the
" public assessment by an actual measurement and computation of
" the produce of the land of each individual. The practice has
" long been entirely discontinued, and we are satisfied that the most
" experienced and capable of the revenue officers would deem the
" revival of it an evil; burthensome, and oppressive to the people,
" and unproductive of any substantial benefit to the pecuniary inte-
" rests of the state."

* See Sir T. Munro's Letter, " Revenue Selections," p. 89 and 91.

surveyed, the process would seem to be much
more elaborate and difficult ; and, as " the curnum's accounts are always false," it is found
necessary to have recourse to various indirect
modes of proceeding for the purpose of acquiring the necessary information with respect to the
land, and the situation and circumstances of the
cultivators.

" *The chief obstacles in the way of it, (a set-
" tlement with the individual cultivators,) arise
" from false accounts, from doubts concerning
" the rate of assessment, and from the difficulty
" of ascertaining the condition of the poorer
" ryots. There is, perhaps, no curnum who in any
" one year ever gives a perfectly true statement
" of the cultivation of his village; and it is only
" the fear of removal or suspension that can make
" him give such accounts as are tolerably accu-
" rate. The proper rate of assessment is found
" either by reference to the accounts of former
" years, or by comparison with the rent of lands
" of the same quality, which have long been
" nearly stationary; and the condition of the
" poorer ryots is learned from the concurring tes-
" timony of their neighbours, who, at the same
" time, will not exaggerate their poverty, lest the
" re-

* See Sir T Munro's Letter, " Revenue Selections," pages 89
and 91.

s

" remissions which may in consequence be grant-
" ed, should fall upon themselves. A short ex-
" planation of what takes place in the Kulwar
" settlement of a single district or tehsildarry,
" will equally apply to the whole number of dis-
" tricts forming a collectorate. I shall here speak
" of a district *in its ordinary state of prosperity*;
" not of one that has been reduced below it, by
" war or any other calamity."

" A district paying a revenue of fifty thousand
" pagodas, usually contains about a hundred
" villages, differing greatly in extent and pro-
" duce; some of them not paying more than a
" hundred pagodas, and others as much as five
" thousand, annual rent. Every village has
" within itself a complete establishment of here-
" ditary revenue servants : a potail to direct the
" cultivation, realise the rent, and manage its
" affairs in general ; a curnum to keep the ac-
" counts ; and a certain number of peons to act
" under the potail, in collecting the kists from
" the ryots. When the ploughing season begins,
" the potail ascertains what land each ryot can
" cultivate ; he permits those who may have met
" with losses, to relinquish a part of their land,
" which he distributes to others who may be wil-
" ling to take it ; and to such as require none
" he continues their former land. He does not
" fix their rents, because this is done by the col-
" lector,

" lector, *when the season is so far advanced that*
" *a judgment can be formed of the crop;* but he
" assures them that their respective rents will
" continue the same as last year, only making
" allowance for such alterations as may become
" unavoidable, from the total revenue of the
" village being somewhat raised or lowered by
" the collector : they are satisfied with this pro-
" mise, receive *betel* from him as a confirmation
" of it, and yoke their ploughs. Specific written
" engagements cannot be made with them at this
" early period of the year, because, as in annual
" settlements, where the failure of the crop is
" great, remissions must be allowed, so where
" the produce is uncommonly abundant, *increase*
" *must be taken to balance such failures,* because
" the potail having relations and friends in the
" village to whom he would be partial, could not
" be safely entrusted with the power of fixing
" rents ; and because the ryots themselves will
" not in this year agree to pay the same rent in
" the ensuing one, lest they should meet with
" losses, which would be aggravated by a rent
" which they might then be unable to bear.
" The tehsildar goes round his district in the
" early part of the season ; his business is chiefly
" to regulate cultivation in those villages where
" it is mismanaged from the incapacity of the
" potail, or impeded by disputes among the prin-

s 2   " cipal

" cipal ryots, and to make advances to the poorer
" sort for the purchase of seed, ploughs, or cattle.
" He also ascertains what land each ryot has
" already cultivated, or engaged to cultivate, du-
" ring the year, which he does by assembling the
" ryots in their respective villages, and examining
" them in the presence of the potails and cur-
" nums ; and accounts of the lands occupied and
" unoccupied, are taken by his cutcherry, which
" accompanies him. He goes round again when
" the crops are ripening, to see their condition,
" and to ascertain whether the quantity of land
" actually cultivated is more or less than that
" which the ryots had engaged to take."

" The collector sets out on his circuit in Sep-
" tember or October when the early crops begin
" to be reaped, and the late ones to be sown. On
" arriving in a district, he assembles all the ryots
" of the four or five nearest villages. The first
" business is to learn how far the cultivation of
" the present year is more or less than that of the
" last ; this is soon done by the help of the
" tehsildar's and curnum's accounts, compared
" with the reports of the potails and ryots.
" Where there is a decrease, it is commonly owing
" to deaths, emigration, or loss of cattle ; where
" there is an increase, it is usually derived from
" new settlers, or additional lands being occu-
" pied by the old ones. In the case of decrease,
" the

" the rent of the lands thrown up is deducted
" from the settlement of last year; in that of
" increase, the rent of the land newly occupied is
" added; and in both cases, the rent of the re-
" maining lands remains the same as before. The
" rent of the land newly occupied is determined
" by the accounts of what it was in former times;
" or, if such accounts cannot be procured, by the
" opinions of the most intelligent ryots; but the
" full rent of waste land is not exacted, until it
" has been in cultivation from two to seven years.
" The number of years, and the gradational rise
" in each year, depend upon the nature of the
" land, and the custom of the village. They
" are known to all parties; and all doubts are
" removed by their being detailed in a proclama-
" tion, or cowle-namah, under the collector's
" seal, circulated to every village.

   " If the cultivation is the same as last year's,
" and no failures occur among the ryots, the rents
" remain unaltered; if the crops are bad, and it
" appears that some of the poor ryots must have
" a remission, the loss, or part of it, *is assessed*
" *upon the lands of the rest,* where it can be done
" without causing any material inconvenience.

   " This assessment never exceeds ten or twelve
" per cent., and is much oftener relinquished
" than carried into effect. In cases where it can
" be easily borne, it is frequently agreed to with-
                        " out

" out difficulty ; and if opposition is made, it is
" generally soon got over by the mediation of the
" ryots of the neighbouring villages present.
" These discuss the point in question with the
" ryots of the objecting village; tell them that
" it is the custom of the country ; use such other
" arguments as may be applicable to the subject ;
" and never fail in persuading them to accede to
" the demand, unless it is really too high, in
" which event it is lowered. Whenever indivi-
" duals, or villages, object to their rent, it is
" always the most expeditious and satisfactory
" way of settling the dispute, to refer it to the
" ryots of other villages, who do more on such
" occasions in half an hour, than a collector and
" his cutcherry in a whole year."

My wish is not to exaggerate ; but when I
find a system requiring a multiplicity of instruments, surveyors, and inspectors ; assessors, ordinary and extraordinary ; potails, curnums, tehsildars, and cutcherry servants ; and when I read
the description given of these officers by the most
zealous advocates of the system, their periodical
visitations are pictured in my imagination as the
passage of a flight of locusts, devouring in their
course the fruits of the earth. For such complicated details, the most select agency would be
required ; whereas the agency which we can command, is represented to be of the most questionable

able character. We do not merely require experience and honesty to execute *one great undertaking ;* the work is ever beginning and never ending, and calls *for a perennial stream of intelligence and integrity.* And can it be doubted, that the people are oppressed and plundered by these multiform agents? The principle of the settlement is to take one-third of the gross produce on account of Government ; and, in order to render the assessment moderate, Sir T. Munro proposed to grant a considerable deduction from the rates deducible from the survey reports. But if it *be* moderate, how does it happen that the people continue in the same uniform condition of labouring peasants? Why do not the same changes take place here as in other communities? One man is industrious, economical, prudent, or fortunate ; another is idle, wasteful, improvident, or unlucky. In the ordinary course of things, one should rise and the other fall : the former should, by degrees, absorb the possessions of the latter ; should become rich, while his neighbour remained poor ; gradations in society should take place ; and, in the course of time, we might naturally expect to see the landlord, the yeoman, and the labourer. And what prevents this natural progression? I should answer, the *officers of government.* The fruits of industry are nipt in the bud. If one man produce more than his fellows, there
is

is a public servant at hand, always ready to snatch the superfluity. And, wherefore, then, should the husbandman toil that a stranger may reap the produce?

There are two other circumstances which tend to perpetuate this uniform condition. The ryots have no fixed possession ; they are liable to be moved from field to field : this they sometimes do of their own accord, for the purpose of obtaining land, supposed to be more lightly assessed ; at other times, the land is assigned by lot, with a view to a more equal and impartial distribution of the good and the bad, among the different cultivators. But these evolutions tend to destroy all local attachments, and are evidently calculated to take away one great incentive to exertion.

The other levelling principle is to be found in the rule, which requires that the ryot shall make good the deficiencies of his neighbour to the extent of ten per cent. ; that is, to the extent, probably, of his *whole surplus earnings.* Of what avail is it that the husbandman be diligent, skilful, and successful, if he is to be mulcted for his neighbour's negligence, or misfortune ? A must pay the debt of B. If a village be prosperous, it matters little, for the next village may have been exposed to some calamity ; and, from the abundance of the one, we exact wherewithal

to

to supply the deficiency of the other.* Is it possible to fancy a system better calculated to baffle the efforts of the individual, to repress industry, to extinguish hope, and to reduce all to one common state of universal pauperism?

It may be asked, is there not a poor and labouring peasantry to be seen under the zemindarry system? Most assuredly there is. In every country a large part of the population must be in the condition of labourers; but the zemindar has an interest in protecting and conciliating his ryot, or he will migrate to another estate. If a scarcity unhappily occur, he has an interest in assisting to preserve the existence of the peasant, and in replacing the seed which his necessities may have compelled him to consume, in order that the deficiency of one season may not be aggravated in the next; and he probably will have the means of furnishing such assistance, for he will, in general, be in possession of a stock of grain, the superfluity of preceding harvests. What store

---

* It may be said, that if one tax fail, it is usual for Governments (and our own among the rest) to substitute another; but there is no analogy between this case and that where an individual is compelled to pay the debt of his neighbour. It is but justice to the Court of Directors to mention, that their minds seem to have revolted at the proposition; and the Board of Revenue at Madras proposed to dispense with the rule; but Sir T. Munro remained firm in the opinion that it was necessary. What must that system be which requires such a rule!

T

store can the labouring peasant be expected to hoard up? Is he not likely to be relieved of his surplus produce by the officers of Government, either on the plea of making good the failure of his neighbours, or to administer to their own avarice? What capital can *he* accumulate? The larger proprietors *may* accumulate; and they have the means of bestowing, and a motive for bestowing, a pittance upon their poorer dependents. The stipendiary servants of the Government have no such motive. They are liable to be removed from their situations from day to day; they have no permanent interest in the prosperity of the district in which they happen to be employed: their object is, generally, to make the most of their situations during the term of their precarious tenure.

I shall only notice one other peculiarity of the " *Ryotwar*" System; under it, say the Board of Revenue, " the ryot was not allowed, on pay-
" ment even of the high survey assessment fixed
" on each field, to cultivate only those fields to
" which he gave the preference; his task was
" assigned to him; he was constrained to occupy
" all such fields as were allotted to him by the
" revenue officers; and, whether he cultivated
" them or not, he was, as Mr. Thackeray empha-
" tically terms it, *saddled* with the rent of each.
" To use the words of Mr. Chaplin, the collector
of

" of Bellary, one of the most able of Colonel
" Munro's former assistants, and still one of the
" most strenuous advocates for the ' Ryotwar '
" system, it was the custom under it to exert, in
" a great degree, the authority which is incom-
" patible with the existing regulations, of *com-*
" *pelling* the inhabitants to cultivate a quantity
" of ground proportionate to their circumstances.
" This he explains to have been done by '*the*
" *power to confine and punish*' them, exercised by
" the collector and his native revenue servants :
" and he expressly adds, that, if the ryot was
" driven by these oppressions from the fields
" which he tilled, it was the established practice
" to *follow the fugitive wherever he went,* and,
" by *assessing him at discretion,* to deprive him
" of all advantage that he might expect to derive
" from a change of residence."*

If forced residence and compulsory service be
essential to the success of the " *Ryotwar,*" or
any other system of revenue administration, this
single fact ought to call for its unqualified con-
demnation. In vain shall we profess moderation,
justice, and humanity, or pretend to be actuated
by an enlightened policy, if a practice be tole-
rated which places our agricultural population in
the condition of Russian or Polish serfs in the
most

* See " Revenue Selections," p. 942.

most barbarous age. I feel interested in uphold-
ing the credit of our Indian administration ; but
no plea of necessity can justify, no pretence
of expediency can excuse, a species of coer-
cion, alike revolting to all good feeling, sub-
versive of personal freedom, and at variance with
all sound principle. Is this a " *native usage,*"
which we are so vehemently called upon to re-
establish? Is this a practice so congenial with
the feelings and the habits of the people, that it
cannot safely be dispensed with ? And is this a
part of the consecrated machinery which Lord
Cornwallis is reproached for having broken to
pieces? This system is not only to be continued
where it already exists ; but it is understood that
the public authorities in this country contemplate
its extension to our western provinces under the
government of Bengal, where *it will be an innovation,* and where it must encounter the opposition of an irritated and warlike people.*

The

* It may be imagined that the peasantry will be well pleased to hold
the lands which they cultivate *direct from the Government ;* but the
alternative presented to their minds will be this: " shall we continue under our native chiefs, to whom we are attached, and who
protect us—or shall we place ourselves under revenue officers, whom
we detest, and who will oppress us ?" What would have been the
election of a Scotch Highlander a century ago, if this alternative
had been presented to him? In fact, the " *ryotwar* " question re-
solves itself into this—whether a stipendiary agency (probably corrupt) shall be employed between the Government and the peasantry—
or whether we shall interpose a proprietary between Government and

the

The Board of Revenue at Fort St. George sum up the character of the " *Ryotwar*" system in the following very forcible language :—

" Ignorant of the true resources of the newly-
" acquired countries, as of the precise nature of
" their landed tenures, we find a small band of
" foreign conquerors no sooner obtaining pos-
" session of a vast extent of territory, peopled
" by various nations, differing from each other in
" language, customs and habits, than they at-
" tempt what would be deemed a Herculean task,
" or rather a visionary project, even in the most
" civilized countries of Europe, of which every
" statistical information is possessed, and of
" which the government are one with the people,
" *viz.,* to fix a land-rent, not on each province,
" district, or country ; not on each estate or farm ;
" but on *every separate field* in their dominions.
" In pursuit of this supposed improvement, we
" find them unintentionally dissolving the ancient
" ties, the ' ancient usages,' which united the
" republic of each Hindoo village, and by a kind
" of Agrarian law, newly assessing and parcel-
" ling out the lands which, from time imme-
" morial, had belonged to the village commu-
" nity collectively ; not only among the indi-
" vidual

the cultivator of the soil. In Bengal, such a proprietary is found to exist, and one chief object of the present publication is to call the attention of the public authorities to the *injustice*, the *impolicy*, and the *danger* of displacing it in our " Ceded and Conquered provinces."

142

" vidual members of the privileged order (the
" Meerassidars and Cadeems), but even among
" the inferior tenantry (the Pyacarries) : we ob-
" serve them ignorantly denying, and by their
" denial, abolishing, *private property in the land* ;
" resuming what belonged to a public body (the
" grama manium), and conferring, in lieu of it,
" a stipend in money on one individual ; profes-
" sing to limit their demand on each field, and, in
" fact, by establishing for such limit an unat-
" tainable maximum, *assessing the ryot at dis-*
" *cretion ;* and, like the Mussulman government
" which preceded them, binding the ryot by force
" to the plough, compelling him to till land ac-
" knowledged to be over-assessed, dragging him
" back to it if he absconded, deferring their de-
" mand upon him until his crop came to matu-
" rity, then taking from him all that could be
" obtained, and leaving to him nothing but his
" bullocks and his seed-grain ; nay, perhaps,
" obliged to supply him even with these, in order
" to renew his melancholy task of cultivating,
" *not for himself, but for them.*"*

To this picture I must add the *delineation given
of the same original by Mr. R. Fullerton,* who
witnessed and condemned the system, and with his
colleague, Mr. Hodgson, manfully but unsuccess-
fully opposed its introduction at Fort St. George.

Extract

* See " Revenue Selections," pages 942 and 943.

Extract from an unrecorded memoir by Mr. Fullerton, written in 1823.

" To convey to the mind of an English reader
" even a slight impression of the nature, opera-
" tion, and results of the *ryotwar* system of reve-
" nue, connected with the judicial arrangements
" of 1816, must be a matter of some difficulty.
" Let him, in the first place, imagine the whole
" landed interest, that is, all the landlords of
" Great Britain, and even the capital farmers, at
" once swept away from off the face of the earth ;
" let him imagine a cess or rent fixed on every
" field in the kingdom, seldom under, generally
" above, its means of payment ; let him imagine
" the land so assessed lotted out to the villagers,
" according to the number of their cattle and
" ploughs, to the extent of forty or fifty acres
" each! Let him imagine the revenue, rated as
" above, leviable through the agency of a hundred
" thousand revenue officers, collected or remitted
" at their discretion, according to their idea of
" the occupant's means of paying, whether from
" the produce of his land or his separate pro-
" perty. And in order to encourage every man
" to act as a spy on his neighbour, and report his
" means of paying, that he may eventually save
" himself from extra demand, let him imagine all
" the cultivators of a village liable at all times to
" a separate demand, in order to make up for the
                                            " failure

" failure of one or more individuals of their
" parish. Let him imagine collectors to every
" county acting under the orders of a board, on
" the avowed principle of destroying all compe-
" tition for labour by a general equalization
" of assessment ; seizing and sending back run-
" aways to each other. And lastly, let him
" imagine the collector the sole magistrate or
" justice of the peace of the county, through the
" medium and instrumentality of whom alone
" any criminal complaint of personal grievance,
" suffered by the subject, can reach the superior
" courts. Let him imagine at the same time
" every subordinate officer, employed in the col-
" lection of the land revenue, to be a police officer,
" vested with power to fine, confine, put in the
" stocks, and *flog*, any inhabitant within his
" range, on any charge, without oath of the ac-
" cuser, or sworn recorded evidence on the case.
" If the reader can bring his mind to contemplate
" such a course, he may then form some judg-
" ment of the civil administration in progress of
" re-introduction into the territories under the
" Presidency of Madras, containing 125,000
" square miles, and a population of twelve
" millions."*

The

* I am indebted to Mr. Hodgson for the document from which
the above extract is taken, as well as for much useful information
regarding the revenue administration at Fort St. George.

The rigours of the system were, no doubt, softened in many instances by the good sense and proper feeling of the ministerial officers who were employed in its execution, and Sir T. Munro himself has always been an advocate for moderation in the assessment. The judicial regulations which were introduced into the Madras territory in 1802 and 1806, were also calculated to impose some salutary restraints upon the revenue servants; but still it is unwise to place in the hands of public functionaries a dangerous instrument, which, if not always used with prudence and forbearance, must become the source of mischief.

The "*ryotwar*" system seems for a time to have given place in some of the Madras districts to "village settlements," which appear to me to have had much to recommend them to a preference, in those instances where a superior order of landholders was not found to exist; but the "*ryotwar*" has once more obtained the ascendancy, and is become the prevailing fashion of the day.

In the quotations which I have given, let it not be supposed that I have selected partial extracts for the purpose of exhibiting an unfair and unfavourable view of a particular system. I could wish that every thing which has been writ-

u   ten

ten in support of it, were submitted to the public. I have studied it in the writings of its warmest advocates : I have sought for an illustration of its defects in their pages ; and to this source I appeal for those facts, which, in my judgment, must determine its true character. I have, it is true, given only a sketch of its leading features. To discuss it thoroughly, much more ample materials must be brought together ; but this will, I trust, be done ; and I have the satisfactory assurance that the work is in excellent hands.*

It remains for me to notice some arrangements which have been judged necessary, or expedient, as auxiliary to the *" ryotwar"* system: and I shall then proceed to deduce its practical effects in a financial point of view.

1st. The collectors of the land revenue at Fort
St.

" Mr. J. Hodgson, late member of council at Fort St. George, who, with his colleague, Mr. Fullerton, so ably opposed the " *ryotwar* " system abroad, is likely, I hope, to bring the merits of the question fully and fairly before the public in this country. I could only pretend to give an outline, without losing sight of my main object; but that outline will, I trust, be completely filled up. In the mean time, I beg to refer to the minute of the Board of Revenue at Fort St. George, bearing date the 5th January 1818, " Revenue Selections," pages 885 and 951, as containing a full exposition of the " ryotwar" system, and of the revenue administration at that Presidency, generally.

St. George have been re-invested with the office
of magistrate in their respective districts.

2d. The tehsildars, or native officers employed
in collecting the land revenue, have been invested
with powers to act as officers of police.

3d. These tehsildars have, by Regulation IV.
of 1821, been empowered to impose fines, and to
inflict corporal punishment.

4th. Seven or eight of the zillah, or district
courts, for the administration of civil justice,
have been abolished.

There are situations in which the union of the
offices of collector and magistrate may be convenient ; there are individuals in whose hands the
powers of the two offices may be united with
safety ; and it is unquestionable that the information which the revenue servants possess, with
respect to the people and their concerns, afford
them great facilities as judicial functionaries,
while their numbers are such as to constitute an
efficient police establishment. In the jungle districts, in particular, where both the people and
their chiefs are in a rude, uncivilized state, our
institutions, to be intelligible and suitable, must
be very simple ; and the simplest form of administration is, no doubt, that which places all
power in the hands of a single individual.

But it is also true that this combination of
power may lead to great abuse; that it holds

u 2   out

out a temptation to abuse ; and that it secures
impunity to the corrupt or tyrannical officer, who
deviates from the path of duty. As a system, it
is dangerous : and whatever may be its practical
usefulness in particular instances, its general application cannot be justified upon any sound
principles.

Regulation IV. of 1821, of the Madras Government, empowers the tehsildars to impose fines, and
to inflict corporal punishment for theft and petty
misdemeanours : and although the correction is
limited to six strokes of the rattan for each
offence, the power to inflict corporal punishment,
however slight, involves the power to inflict *disgrace ;* and this, in India, where the better classes
are extremely sensitive in all matters affecting
reputation, is liable to be applied to the very
worst purposes.

It is by no means my intention to assert that
the authority of magistrate was given to invigo-
rate and uphold the *" ryotwar"* system, or to
strengthen the hands of the *"tehsildar"* in his
revenue capacity. It was honestly given with
very different views : but when a public officer,
exercising two functions, is seen armed with the
fasces, it requires very nice discrimination to determine in what quality they are intended to be
used ; and, certainly, no prudent man would oppose the will of an officer so fatally armed, should

it

it occur to him to enforce a revenue exaction by
the threat of a summary judicial process. That
the tehsildars have ample powers to do mischief,
cannot be doubted, and that they will exert their
power for corrupt and oppressive purposes, cannot be doubted by those who do not discredit the
description which has been given of those functionaries.

Nor is it intended by me to affirm that the
abolition of the zillah, or district courts of justice,
had for its object to afford the revenue servants
freer scope for their operations ; but I do apprehend that such must inevitably be the consequence of their suppression. They were abolished,
partly " for the sake of public economy," and
partly, because Sir T. Munro seems disposed to
consider those courts as the source of inconvenience, if not a positive evil. He observes, " but
" whatever mode of settlement may be finally
" adopted, the inhabitants, but particularly the
" ryots, must suffer great inconvenience, and even
" distress, from the judicial regulations, as they
" now stand. The evils which they are likely
" to increase rather than to diminish, are delay,
" vexation, bribery wrong decisions.* The
                                    " delay

* A man of a dull understanding may be consistent in error. A
man of talents, like Sir T. Munro, is not likely to continue so, for
the " experimentum crucis " brings him back, sooner or later, to
the

" delay will necessarily arise from the forms,
" which not only the judge, but the native com-
" missioners must adhere to in their proceedings,
" and from all the principal, and a great part of
" even the petty suits, being brought before the
" judge."* &c. &c.

To this opinion, I must oppose one of the
highest authority on all questions relating to the
administration of justice in India—Sir Henry
Strachey, whose experience and attainments give
to his opinions a genuine value, and whose candour and independent mind assure us that we
have always his unbiassed sentiments, thus expresses himself.

" My opinion of the judicial administration
" established in Bengal, and the provinces de-
" pending upon it, is on the whole very favour-
" able. To the system itself, the institution of
" the

the right road. As an illustration of this remark, I will quote a
passage from the report of Sir T. M. and Mr. Stratton in 1818, on
the Zillah Courts.

" If not a single original suit were to come before them (the
Zillah Courts), they would still be of the most essential use to the
country as Courts of Appeal and Criminal Courts; and still more,
perhaps, by the salutary check which they would maintain over the
districts and village moonsifs, by which they would compel them
to perform properly those subordinate judicial duties, which can by
no other agents be so conveniently discharged." Upon what ground,
I ask, are these courts to be abolished? I understand that in one
instance, the native inhabitants have themselves protested against
the abolition—and with reason, no doubt.

* See " Revenue Selections," page 105, *et seq.*

" the courts of justice, formed as they are upon
" the English model, and the rules by which they
" are guided, I see no material objection."

" If the ' ryotwar' plan can be carried on suc-
" cessfully after the establishment of the judicial
" authorities ; if rules can be framed, under
" which the ryotwar collector shall act as manager
" only of an estate, and the judge shall have the
" usual power of redressing grievances, *then* I
" shall not condemn the plan ; but I protest
" against the ryotwar collector having any judi-
" cial power whatever. As manager of an estate
" only he ought to be considered ; consequently,
" we must be jealous of his power, lest he should
" pervert it to purposes of extortion. Every
" manager of an estate has, in India, a natural
" inclination or tendency towards extortion. If
" any man, whose business it is to collect rent
" from the ryots, shall persuade himself that,
" while so occupied, he is the fittest person in the
" world to defend these ryots from the oppres-
" sions which he and his dependents commit, that
" his occupation supersedes the necessity of all
" control, that person, in my opinion, most
" grossly errs."*

Mr. T. H. Ernst, another judicial servant of
great experience, writes as follows.

" One

* See " Judicial Selections," pages 52, 64, and 65.

" One of the most important benefits which the
" natives have derived from it," (the judicial
system) " is the security which it has afforded them
" in their persons. They are no longer beat and
" tortured, and imprisoned, as they used to be,
" by the officers employed in the collections, and
" by their private creditors ; and this very ma-
" terial change in their condition should never be
" lost sight of in discussing the merits of the
" present system."*

Mr.

* See " Judicial Selections," page 31. The following extracts exhibit another contrast between the opinions of Sir T. Munro and
Sir H. Strachey.

Extract from a Memorandum by Colonel Munro, on the Judicial
System : page 105, vol. ii, " Judicial Selections."

" In the various plans that have been suggested for reducing the
public expenditure, none seem to have been thought of for lessening
that of the Judicial Department, though there is none in which re-
trenchment may be made with more advantage both to Government
and the inhabitants." &c. &c.

" In a civilized populous country, like India, justice can be well
dispensed only through the agency of the natives themselves. It is
absurd to suppose, that they are so corrupt as to be altogether unfit
to be intrusted with the discharge of this important duty," &c &c.

Extract from Sir Henry Strachey's Answer to the Questions put
by the Court of Directors in 1813 : page 72, vol. ii, " Judicial Selections."

" It is, I should hope, superfluous to consider the native system :
we cannot seriously talk of reviving it in Bengal : what we have
done cannot be revoked. We have produced great changes, and,
occasionally, done some mischief, which cannot easily be repaired.
But barbarism and confusion will, I am sure, overwhelm the country,
if we give up our system now, and throw the natives suddenly upon
their own resources."

" With

Mr. Ravenshaw, also, expresses himself in the following emphatic terms.

" In saying thus much, I beg I may not be
" understood as deprecating the system itself,
" for I have no hesitation in pronouncing, that
" our present Indian constitution is the proudest
" monument of wisdom ever erected in India ;
" that the regulations, as they stand at present,
" are capable of rendering the system in time in a
" great measure fit and efficient : that they re-
" quire only a few alterations and additions to
" make it as perfectly so as human institutions
" can be ; and that when the full benefits of it
" are generally felt as well as seen, the natives
" will consider it as the greatest blessing ever
" conferred on them.

" So far from thinking the expense of the pre-
" sent system could with propriety be diminished,
" either by *reducing the number of courts* or
" the scale of establishment, I am decidedly of
" opinion that, if the expense could be borne,
" great

" With all the abuses and want of skill that are visible in our
system, it displays, I firmly believe, more of intellect and rationality,
and consequently of substantial justice, than can be found in the
policy and legislation of the whole eastern world, from Constantino-
ple to China. It would be unpardonable to withhold these blessings,
which a series of astonishing events has enabled England to dispense to Hindostan."

x

" great advantage would be derived from *increas-*
" *ing* the number of courts."*

It would not be difficult to multiply authorities,
for the purpose of shewing that the judicial powers
cannot generally be intrusted to the revenue servants with safety, and that the courts of justice,
although not perfectly free from objections, and
not yet harmonizing with the notions and habits
of the natives, cannot be dispensed with, without
exposing the people to very great oppression.
But, let Sir T. Munro himself describe the state of
a country, where the " native institutions," so
highly vaunted, have had full scope and effect,
unfettered by English courts of law.

" A very large proportion of the talliars* are
" themselves thieves; all the kawillgars* are
" themselves robbers exempting them, and many
" of them are murderers ; and, though they are
" now afraid to act openly, there is no doubt
" that many of them still secretly follow their for-
" mer practices. Many potails and curnums,
" also, harbour thieves ; so that no traveller can
" pass

* See " Judicial Selections," pages 131 to 135. There is an
able minute on the subject, by Mr. Fullerton, from which I should
quote largely, if I were not unwilling to extend this Essay beyond
its more immediate object. I should also refer to the opinions of
Lord Teignmouth, of the Marquess of Wellesley, and of the Government of Fort St. George, in 1812: as well as to the report of
the Select Committee of the House of Commons, on the merits of
our judicial system.

" pass through the ceded districts without being
" robbed, who does not employ either his own
" servants, or those of the village, to watch at
" night; and even this precaution is very often
" ineffectual. Many offenders are taken, but
" great numbers also escape, for connivance must
" be expected among the kawillgars and the
" talliars, who are themselves thieves; and the
" inhabitants are often backward in giving infor-
" mation, from the fear of *assassination, which
" was formerly very common,* and sometimes hap-
" pens on such occasions."*

It has been said, and very justly, I admit, that
the natives of India are attached to their usages
and institutions ; but they are an intelligent
people, and although they may be incommoded
by the forms and process of our courts, to which
they are not yet familiarized, they are fully sensible of the value of British protection, and it is
impossible to believe that they can be attached to
the state of anarchy described in the foregoing
extract.

Sir T. Munro is too much of a statesman not

to

* See " Judicial Selections," pages 220, 221, *et seq*. The kawill-
gar was a head-officer of police under the native administration.
" The talliar acts under the potail of the village; and the potail
" under the Amildar of the district; but all these persons are, at
" least, as much *revenue* as police-officers. The talliar and potail
" hold their offices by inheritance."

to be aware that no society can exist without civil institutions ; and after enlarging upon the defects and insufficiency of our judicial system, he proceeds to explain the native system of judicature, which he considers us to have displaced, and which it has been his object to re-establish.

Para. 24. " It is to be feared that no complete " remedy for these evils can be found ; but the " most effectual one would be to resort to the " trial by jury, termed by the inhabitants ' *pun-* " *chayet,*' or *subba,* according to their respective " languages. The judicial code in civil cases " authorizes trial by referees, arbitrators and " munsifs ; but it says nothing of trial by ' *Pun-* " *chayet.*' It seems strange that this code, which " has been framed expressly for the benefit of the " natives, should omit entirely the only mode of " trial which is general and popular among them, " and regarded as fair and legal ; for there can " be no doubt that the trial by ' punchayet ' is " as much the common law of India, in civil mat- " ters, as that by jury in England. No native " thinks that justice is done where it is not " adopted ; and in appeals of causes formerly " settled, whether under a native government, or " under that of the Company, previous to the " establishment of the courts, the reason assign- " ed, in almost every instance, was, that the de- " cision was not given by a ' *punchayet,*' but

by

" by a public officer, or by persons acting under
" his influence, or sitting in his presence. The
" native who has a good cause, always applies
" for a ' *punchayet*,' while he who has a bad one
" seeks the decision of a collector or a judge,
" because he knows that it is easier to deceive
" them. It may be objected that a ' *pun-*
" *chayet*' has no fixed constitution ; that the
" number of its members may vary from five to
" fifty, or even more, and that its verdicts are
" often capricious. But all these objections for-
" merly lay against juries, and they might un-
" questionably be removed from ' *punchayets* '
" by future improvements."*

The " *punchayet* "† is an assembly of arbitrators ; and, although it had fallen much into disuse
in most of the Bengal districts, it was never intended by our Government to suppress it. On
the contrary, the judicial code expressly encouraged appeals to arbitration, and the people
have always been perfectly free to use the
" punchayet," whenever they were mutually disposed to give it a preference. It was, however,
judged

* See " Revenue Selections," page 106.
† See Appendix C, on the origin and nature of " *Punchayet*,"
by H. T. Colebrooke, Esq., than whom there can be no higher authority on questions of Hindoo law and Hindoo institutions. This
brief Memoir should satisfy those who have been accustomed to
regard the " *Punchayet*" as constituting the entire system of Hindoo
judicature, that they have been entirely in a mistake.

judged necessary to render awards liable to be set
aside for corruption, and this enactment operated,
no doubt, to discourage individuals of respec-
tability from undertaking the office of arbitrator ;
it in consequence gradually declined in the es-
timation of the people, and there is reason
perhaps to regret that an institution of the kind
could not have been secured from abuse by means
short of those which appear to have occasioned
its disuse.

As an auxiliary to a regular system of judicature, the " *punchayet* " may be found extremely
useful. It was in general resorted to for the
purpose of settling questions relating to caste,
professional privileges and usages, the customs
of merchants, and the like ; and it might be employed, quite as usefully, in adjusting boundary
disputes, questions between landlord and tenant,
and simple contracts generally. But as a system
standing alone and unsupported, its incompetency
must at once be apparent. How is it possible for
such an assembly to stand as a bulwark between
Government, or its officers, and the people ? How
could such an assembly be called upon to decide
an intricate question of inheritance, or any question whose solution should depend upon a knowledge of the general principles of law ? To
maintain that it is all-sufficient, and adequate to
all the ends of justice, would be as unreasonable
as

as to contend that it can never be used with advantage.*

Sir John Malcolm, in his " Memoir on Central India," has given a particular account of the " *punchayet,*" and his opinions are strongly in favour of the institution. The Hon. Mountstuart Elphinstone, in his " Report† on the Territories conquered from the Peishwa," gives, also, a fair and impartial description of it, and delineates its merits and defects with a clear and just discrimination. From these and other authorities, there are satisfactory grounds for concluding that the " *Punchayet,*" as a court of arbitration, acting *with consent of parties,* ought to be sustained and countenanced by the Government wherever it is found to exist; and that, as such, it is likely to prove a very useful engine in the administration of justice. It is, however, an institution rather suited to a rude state of society, in which friends and neighbours are naturally called in to arbitrate differences between individuals; but it would seem to be scarcely adapted to a more advanced stage of civilization, when, the concerns of the community becoming complex and multifarious, written

* In a short Memoir which I wrote in India some fifteen years ago on our judicial system, I recommended the use of the " *punchayet* " in a modified shape; so that I have no prejudices to overcome on this subject.

† See Report, printed in Calcutta in 1821.

ten laws are found necessary, and nicer distinctions must be made in the administration of those laws.

The advocates of the " *punchayet* " may perhaps be surprised to learn that their favourite institution has been tried upon a large scale in modern times, and that the experiment is considered entirely to have failed.

The first National Assembly of France, by a law of the 24th August 1790, which was followed by many subsequent enactments in the same spirit, decreed that " arbitration afforded the " means the most reasonable for settling suits " between citizens ;" and this principle having obtained high favour for the time, it was every where extended, and found its way into the legislation of the remote Cantons of Switzerland. It was applied even to cases of inheritance, and " *dans cette manie d'arbitrage,*" observes M. Bellot,* " on alla plus oin ; le mot de *juge cessa* " *d'être un terme légal ;* on ne reconnut plus que " des arbitres volontaires, ou des *arbitres publics,* " selon qu'ils étaient nommés par les parties, ou " par les assemblées électorales."

But what was the result of this expulsion of the very name of judge from the judicial code?

" L'ex-

* See " Exposé des Motifs de la Loi sur la procédure Civile, pour le Canton de Genève," par P. F. Bellot.

" L'expérience mit bientôt à découvert les
" vices de ce systême ; et une voix générale ac-
" cusa l'imprévoyance du législature.

" De toutes parts on citait en France des sen-
" tences arbitrales, où les lois avaient été im-
" pudemment violées, les intérêts les plus sacrés
" compromis ; où dès arbitres ignorans, pusil-
" lanimes, subornés, n'avaient écouté que leurs
" préjugés, la crainte, ou la faveur. Deux ans
" de règne suffirent à l'arbitrage forcé pour ac-
" cumuler plus d'abus que n'en avait présenté
" l'ordre judiciaire dans une longue suite
" d'années.

" Enfin, les tribunaux de famille et l'arbitrage
" forcé, furent supprimés ; et nous détruisîmes, à
" notre tour, l'œuvre d'une imitation servile."

Such was the early fate of the French and the
Swiss " Punchayet ;" but let it not be supposed
that the learned Juris-consult of Geneva condemns
all arbitrations indiscriminately : on the contrary,
he seems to be fully sensible that *voluntary* arbitrations may be resorted to with great advantage, and that provision ought to be made in
every system of judicature for giving proper effect
to this mode of arbitrament between contending
parties.

I have been led into a digression upon the
" *Punchayet,*" in consequence of observing that
expectations have been encouraged with respect

Y   to

to it, which are not likely, I fear, to be realized;
and, in consequence of the disposition which has
been manifested of late, to exaggerate the merits
of the native institutions, and to condemn every
thing which is supposed (however erroneously) to
innovate upon them. Will the warmest advocates
of the " *Punchayet* " pretend that it can protect
the people of India against the Government, or
its revenue officers? And will any person be
found to maintain that they ought not to be
protected? Will it be contended that we ought
not to have written laws? that we ought not to
have courts of justice to administer and enforce
those laws? Or that the people of England
are so ignorant of general principles, have made
such slight advances in knowledge and the
science of legislation, as to be incapable of improving the institutions and jurisprudence of
India, in which *revenue, religion,* and *law,* all
take their places together with scarcely a line
of demarcation between them? Simple, suitable,
and sufficient as these institutions are represented
to be, they are not all alike entitled to our admi-
ration and support ; and, although they ought not
in any case to be hastily subverted, they must be
accommodated to the altered condition of the
people and the peculiar situation of their rulers ;
and it should be the study of the government, as
it unquestionably is its duty, to give to our native
subjects,

subjects, not only the most perfect institutions, which may be compatible with the existing state of society among them, but to model those institutions in such manner that they may operate towards improving the moral, intellectual, and social condition of the population of India.*

I shall

* I am induced to quote the following remarks by Mr. Fullerton on the retrograde movement made at Fort St. George, towards the re-introduction of the native system of administration.

" The whole reasoning and argument of the Honourable the Court of Directors, introducing the late innovations, form one tissue of individual opinion, and few of those individuals quoted were in a station high enough to take a wide and extensive view of the subjects they were discussing: their opinions were generally founded on the narrow and contracted scale of personal feelings under subordinate situations. No Governor, from the days of Lord Cornwallis, and no member of council at any of the Presidencies, has ever questioned the general policy of the judicial system; none have ever proposed the union of executive and judicial powers. In the controul and direction of departments, in which hundreds are employed, they have been placed in a situation to observe the variations of human intellect and propensities, and the results brought about by them in the administration of human affairs: when they contemplated the indolence and inactivity, the no less ruinous effects of the opposite extremes, over zeal of others, the exclusive union of pre-eminent qualities in the few, the partial defects of the many, they are led to consider that system the best which keeps distinct separate powers, and trusts least to individual perfection. The innovations of 1816 had not their origin with the Government of India, they were founded on private opinions: they have been justly resisted in Bengal; and their operation at Madras is certainly against the united opinion of the whole experience of the civil service and civil government there."

Mr. Fullerton further remarks:—

" The institutions of one province were most erroneously supposed

those

I shall now proceed to examine the *fiscal* effects of the "*ryotwar*" system, which not only had the benefit of Sir T. Munro's personal services on its introduction into the ceded and other districts, but which has enjoyed his fostering care as head of the government of Fort St. George ; a situation in which he was, of course, enabled to select for its execution and superintendence, those officers who were best qualified to promote its success.

I regret that my materials are not more complete ; but as the Court of Directors could not, consistently with their rules and practice (the propriety of which I am not at all prepared to dispute),

those of the whole territories under Madras, were reported as such by the individual presiding there; and, on the faith of that individual opinion, were peremptorily ordered to be applied to all other districts, many of which were in quite a different state; the order being peremptory, it became the duty of the local government to make them fit, by requisite alterations, the best way they could; but it naturally enough became the object of the first promoter of the change to make good the pre-asserted grounds for innovation, rather to keep the incongruity out of sight than to admit its existence, and meet it by further arrangements. The remark is not confined to judicial alterations; the whole projected changes in the revenue department, the general introduction of the ryotwar system, are founded on the tenures and occupancy of land in the " Ceded Districts " alone, and the absence of all landed property there; the difference has been since admitted, and it is to be hoped, the error of founding a general system on local circumstances and individual opinions is now discovered."

pute), allow me access to their records and books of account, I have not been able to ascertain with certainty the exact degree in which the occasional failures in the Land revenue of Madras are to be ascribed to the " *ryotwar*" system of administration.

The Honourable Court in their letter to the Bengal Government, bearing date the 14th May 1823, observe generally, " that the land revenues " of Madras have fallen off considerably since " 1813-14 ;" and it is understood that, since the date of this letter, information has been received that remissions will be required at that Presidency in the past year 1823-24, to the extent of from 25 to 32 per cent. on the jumma, or assessment.

But how does it happen that the revenue should be even *stationary* at Madras, when it has advanced so rapidly in the Bengal provinces ? In our " Ceded and Conquered" territory, the revenue has increased in the proportion of about one-third in the course of fourteen years ; and in the districts in which the " permanent settlement" has been concluded, the rents of the landholders are supposed, in many instances, to have doubled, and quadrupled. Of this fact we have strong presumptive evidence in the augmented value of landed property ; and Lord Cornwallis may be said to *have bestowed millions* on the people

people of India, since, prior to the " permanent
settlement," the land had scarcely any saleable
value, whereas at the present day, the rate of
purchase is, perhaps, higher than in most of the
countries of Europe.* Is this the case at Madras?
Can the privilege of cultivating land, the rent of
which it is proposed to raise with the increase of
every blade of corn, become a valuable, or a saleable property ?

And how is the improvement in the Bengal
provinces to be accounted for? Partly from the
stimulus given to industry by the limitation of
the public demand on the land ; partly, from the
greater security of property, which has tended to
promote the accumulation of capital ; partly,
from the existence of large estates (a thing pro-
scribed by the " *ryotwar*" system), the proprietors of which find it their interest to lay out capital in the improvement of their lands; partly,
from the produce of land being in greater demand to supply the consumption of a population
increasing in numbers and in wealth ; and partly,
from the introduction, or extension, of valuable
articles of agricultural produce, such as indigo,
cotton, sugar, and the like.

And why has not the same improvement taken
place in the Madras districts ? Sir T. Munro, in
his

* See Letter from Bengal " Revenue Selections," page 166.

his report on the " Ceded Districts," which were
under his immediate charge, observes as follows :
" It (the statement) was made out in 1211, since
" which period, the proportions of some of the
" more valuable articles, as indigo and sugar,
" have greatly augmented. Indigo to the value
" of star pagodas 1,05,000, paid duty in 1215 ;
" and it is supposed that the export to the Car-
" natic, for which no duty was paid, was equal
" to star pagodas 20,000. The quantity would
" have been nearly doubled in 1216, had not the
" crops been destroyed by the drought. The
" coarse sugar, or jaggery, manufactured in 1216,
" was double the quantity of any preceding year.
" The increase of these articles is occasioned by
" the addition of an extra land-rent, amounting
" to *twice or three times the ordinary rate;* to
" which all land employed in their culture was
" subjected ; and this increase is likely to go on
" progressively, as the demand for them is great.
" Cotton, one of the chief products of the ' Ceded
" Districts,' has not increased in a similar de-
" gree, because the demand for it is not greater
" than usual, and because from its being a com-
" mon article of cultivation, and never having
" paid more than the ordinary land-rent, it has
" obtained no advantage from the equalization
" of rent by the survey."*

These

* See " Revenue Selections," page 120.

These remarks go very far to answer my question, for if an *extra assessment* of *twice* or *three times* the *ordinary rate*, as well as a transit duty, is to be applied whenever a promising article of cultivation makes its appearance, the most effectual means are taken to prevent its introduction, or at least its extension. Some articles may, for a time, succeed in spite of this discouragement; but (although the language is somewhat obscure) we see that cotton, a valuable product, can scarcely bear up against the *ordinary* land-rent; and in fact, if it could yield more, it is quite clear that it would be immediately subjected to a higher rate.

The seasons in the Peninsula may be more irregular than in our Bengal provinces, and the harvest may, in consequence, be more uncertain; the rivers not being navigable, are not calculated to facilitate the internal commerce of the country; and there may be other local circumstances unfavourable to the improvement of the Madras territory. But who can fail to perceive, that the system of revenue administration has much to do in arresting the progress of improvement? Will industry be called into action when the demand of the tax-gatherer keeps pace with its produce? Will capital accumulate where there is no security for property, no law but that which is administered under the auspices of a revenue officer?

Will

Will opulent consumers be found where no capital is allowed to accumulate ? And can any country advance and become prosperous where the land has no saleable value, where there is no motive for laying out capital in its improvement, and where no order of human beings is to be found between the government and the labouring peasant ? Certainly not. The " *permanent settlement* " contains within it a principle of *vitality ;* the " *ryotwar* " system, a principle of *decay.* The one works out a remedy even for the evil of over assessment ; the other, whenever the object of over-assessment, must become its victim.

Let us now compare the revenue realised from the " Ceded Districts," which were settled by Sir T. Munro, with the revenue which has been realised from the " Ceded and Conquered Provinces" under the Bengal Presidency.

Madras—" Ceded Districts."

	1808-9.*	1821-22.	Increase.
Land Revenue, Sayer & Customs, Pags.	17,04,517	18,14,303	1,09,786
= £681,807	725,721	43,914

Bengal—" Ceded and Conquered Provinces :"

	1808-9.	1821-22.	Increase.
Do. do. C.Rups.	3,01,90,334	4,28,81,803	1,26,91,469
= £3,019,033	4,288,180	1,269,146

The

* That I may not be suspected of having taken an unfavourable period for comparison, I subjoin a memorandum of the revenues of the Madras " Ceded Districts " from 1808-9 to the latest period, 1821-22, for which the accounts have been printed. I am aware that these districts were not under " ryotwar" management during the

The " Ceded Districts" of Madras furnish, I
believe, as favourable a specimen as could be
taken, to shew the effects of the "*ryotwar*" sys-'
tem : they are pointed out by the Court of Directors as an instance to prove " that the difficul-
" ties attending the system may be surmounted ;"
they were placed under this system of management soon after the period of their cession ; they
have enjoyed the benefit of select agency ; the
Government itself has countenanced and encouraged the experiment; and the officer with
whom it originated was allowed to model and
apply the system in the manner most likely to
insure its success ; and yet, with all these special
advantages, the land revenue has continued nearly
stationary during fourteen years, while our Bengal provinces, enjoying only the *promise* of a "*permanent settlement*," have yielded, within the same
period,
the whole period, but if they do not furnish a complete specimen of
continued " ryotwar" management, they shew what is to be expected from the unsettled and ever-varying systems adopted from
time to time at Fort St. George.

1808-9 ...	Pagodas17,04,517	1815-16...	Pagodas 17,67,828
1809-10	16,57,103	1816-17	17,82,463
1810-11	17,20,842	1817-18	16,05,774
1811-12	16,21,466	1818-19	18,68,184
1812-13	16,83,575	1819-20	18,10,309
1813-14	17,13,686	1820-21	16,58,753
1814-15	17,13,032	1821-22	18,14,303

If the " Ceded Districts " should not be considered a fair specimen
of " *Ryotwar* " management, let me refer the reader to Appendix D,
where he will find the fiscal effects of this System, exhibited in the
Province of " *Canara*."

period, an increase of annual revenue to the
amount of £1,270,000! A greater contrast could
not well be exhibited, and it would be quite unreasonable to deny that the difference in the two
cases is to be referred, in a very great degree, to
the difference in the system of management.

Had a permanent settlement been concluded in
the Madras districts fourteen years ago, some speculative financier would doubtless now be found
to deplore and to condemn the *improvident sacrifice of revenue*. Lord Cornwallis' settlement (most
unjustly, as I contend) has thus been arraigned ;
but the event has shewn, in the present instance,
that the assumption would have been altogether
gratuitous, for those Mines of Wealth which his
Lordship is reproached for having sacrificed, have
here produced nothing. If we had fixed our
demand on the Madras Ceded Districts, in perpetuity, fourteen years ago, the land, it is true, might
not have yielded more than it does at present; but
the customs and the *"sayer"* would have increased, for the people would have emerged from
a state of pauperism ; the cultivation of the soil
would have been extended ; and with its extension, tangible articles of taxation would have
been found.

We should certainly have sacrificed above a
million of annual revenue, if we had concluded
the permanent settlement of our Bengal " Ceded
and Conquered Provinces" at the same period, for

some of the districts (Goruckpore in particular), were waste, or only partially cultivated; but we have the declaration of the local officers, that many parts of that territory are now arrived at a high state of improvement; and it is extremely doubtful, whether a further delay in fixing the assessment, will be attended with any pecuniary advantage to the government.* Of one fact we may be quite certain from the concurring testimony of the local authorities, that a further delay will be attended with discredit to our name, if it do not excite a spirit of disaffection throughout our western territory. The landholders have received, in the most authentic form, repeated assurances of our intention, to conclude a "permanent settlement" with them; and whatever we may pretend, they can never be made to believe that, in disappointing their just expectations, we have not been actuated by a sordid, rapacious policy. Is it possible, indeed, for them to believe that

* I have learnt, with regret, that, in consequence of a drought, remissions of Revenue are likely to be necessary in these provinces in the present year 1824-25, and I doubt whether we shall hereafter obtain from them the same revenue which they would have yielded if the permanent settlement had been concluded three years ago. I doubt, moreover, whether the remissions now required would have been called for in that case, for the Landholders, under a permanent settlement, could have borne partial losses, and would have had sufficient credit with the Native Bankers, to enable them to advance the public Revenue, even under circumstances of temporary inconvenience to themselves.

that a government, which seems disposed to appropriate a vast territory as *universal landlord*, and to collect, not *revenue* but *rent*, can have any other view than to extract from the people the utmost fraction which they can pay?

The Honourable Court of Directors, in their letter to the supreme Government of the 16th March 1813,* appear to attach great weight to the opinion of the first commissioners who were deputed to form the settlement of the western provinces in 1807; but the objections of those officers did not apply at all to the *principle* of the permanent settlement; they considered the measure, with reference to time and circumstances, to be generally *premature;* but, in two particular instances, they recommended its immediate introduction, and nothing could be more remote from their intentions than to countenance the project of substituting the "*ryotwar*" system of management in any part of our territory.

If we wish to preserve tranquillity in our western provinces, if we wish to secure the ample revenue which they at present yield, if we wish

to

* See "Revenue Selections," page 140, *et seq.* I am anxious, as one of the commissioners, to explain my sentiments on this important question, the decision of which may affect the tranquillity of a valuable portion of our Indian territory. Its tranquillity will not, in my opinion, be long preserved, if the project of sending out a host of surveyors to measure and assess every field be carried into effect, and I understand that steps have already been taken for the execution of this ill-judged project.

to attach to our government, by the strong ties of interest, that class of individuals who possess the most powerful influence over the minds of the people, we shall redeem our pledge, and fix the assessment in perpetuity in all those estates which *" may be in a sufficiently improved state of cultiva- "tion."* In those instances where the lands have not yet been extensively cultivated, it would be advisable, I think, to grant, (preparatory to a permanent settlement,)long leases,or leases for the incumbent's life (if there be no joint proprietors) ; and in the course of twenty years, we should not only have the satisfaction of seeing the country in the highest state of improvement, and the people contented and well affected to our Government, but we should also have it in our power to draw, if necessary, a larger revenue from the land, without imposing burthens disproportionate to its resources.

We have not yet the means of judging, with any degree of certainty, of the probable resources of the country acquired by conquest from the Marhattas in 1818 ; but as the administration of our predecessors appears to have been corrupt and oppressive, we may presume that much time will be required to develope its natural powers, and that the present revenue may admit of considerable

* I quote the words of the Regulation, in which the promise is made to the Landholders.

siderable augmentation under a better system of management. The gross receipts from the territory on the Nurbuddah, immediately dependent upon the Bengal Presidency, have been as follow, in the last three years, viz.

1819-20 .... Current Rupees 20,55,317
1820-21 77,99,088
1821-22 * 60,34,198

The gross receipts from the province of Candeish and the other districts, which were conquered from the Peishwa, and placed under the Bombay government, amounted in 1819-20 to the sum of Current Rupees 78,37,092 ; but, as the revenue of this territory is not separately stated in the accounts of the two last years, I cannot ascertain exactly what progress has been made in calling forth its resources. There is reason, however, to believe, from the increase which has taken place in the *aggregate* receipts at Bombay, that an improvement has already been effected ; and although the increase of military and other charges will necessarily absorb a large portion of the revenue, the new territory is likely to prove a valuable acquisition.

Upon the whole, the land revenue of India may be relied upon generally, as a firm and legitimate resource ; and the only doubts which I entertain of its permanency and productiveness, have reference

* I cannot explain the cause of the decrease in this year.

rence to the system of management which has been adopted in particular quarters. I do not pretend to decide who are, or ought to be, the proprietors of the soil, whether zemindars, talookdars, or malicks, meerassydars, ryots, or the village corporation*; but in every stage of my inquiry I find reason to be satisfied *that the government neither is, nor ought to be, that proprietor.* I am sensible that we ought not to disturb existing institutions without a necessity, or some strong and obvious reason. I am aware that all changes are attended with more or less inconvenience, and sudden and violent changes, with more or less danger ; and that the prospect of improvement ought to be very satisfactory before we determine to innovate upon long-established habits and usages. But if notions and customs, consecrated by their antiquity, are never to be meddled with, why have we discountenanced and

sup-

---

* Consisting of the following personages, some of whom are, however, to be considered rather as servants of the corporation than the corporation itself. They constitute evidently the rudiments of a society, performing those offices which are first called for when men begin to form themselves into communities.

The potail, or head inhabitant,	Goldsmith,
Curnum, or accountant,	Potter,
Barber,	The bard,
Washerman,	Currier,
Carpenter,	Astrologer, or schoolmaster,
Smith,	Watchman.

suppressed the trial by ordeal ? the punishment
for witchcraft—the practice of infanticide, and
other gross superstitions ? The practice of sitting
*dhurna,** was resorted to as an expedient for
enforcing demands where the administration of
public justice was not sufficiently provided for ;
but such a practice ought not surely to be tole-
rated by a government, which is both able and
willing to assist its subjects in asserting their
rights, and in obtaining the redress of their
wrongs ? Is it fitting that the British Government
should regard with unconcern the state of villa-
nage and slavery which exists in the southern and
western parts of the Peninsula, merely because
our Hindoo and Mahomedan predecessors were
indifferent to the condition of those, whom their
anti-social institutions degraded in the scale of
society ? I am not the advocate of innovation ; but
still there are certain principles, whose operation
may always be depended upon : certain feelings
which are common to men in all situations. We
may be quite sure that all men desire to possess
property, and landed property, perhaps, in as
great a degree as any other ; that the more
moderate the demands of the government may
be

* The practice of sitting at the door of a debtor, or supposed
aggressor, without taking food, until some compromise be effected. The ceremony was usually performed by a Bramin, whose
life it would have been criminal to endanger by a refusal to comply
with the demand.

be upon that property, the better pleased will be
its proprietor : that if the demand upon the land
be moderate, the longer it continues to be so,
and the more binding and absolute the pledge for
its continuance, the better satisfied will be the
landholder : in other words, that where the assessment is moderate, long leases will be preferred to a precarious tenure, and perpetuity to
either.* We may also be sure that men do not
covet the visitations of "surveyors," and "public
inspectors," nor take delight in the presence of
the tax-gatherer, *especially if he be armed with
judicial powers;* that they are likely to work
when they are allowed to enjoy the fruits of
their labour; that where industry is encouraged

* The following just remarks are quoted from Captain Briggs, political agent in Candeish. " I am disposed to think that the system
" adopted by Mullick Umber, of making lands over in perpetuity, *is*
" *of great antiquity among the Hindoos,* and was probably once uni-
" formly adopted throughout India. Whenever the Eyen Jumma ap-
" pears to have increased, it has been in consequence of additional
" cultivation, not of an increased rate of assessment, and nothing is
" more favourable to the extension and improvement of agriculture
" than a moderate, but permanent tax, and an interest in the soil.
" The portion remaining to the cultivator should be such as to enable
" him to add indirectly to the wealth of the State; he should not
" only have the means of improving his field and taking in more
" ground, but he should have sufficient left to live in such a way as
" to encourage manufactures and trade, and thus become an indirect
" promoter of the revenue derived from the customs, as it must be
" evident, *where there is no opulence in the people, there can be no
" source from whence revenue can be derived.*"

raged and protected, a country is likely to flourish, and that its prosperity reflects back a real good upon the protecting Government. The mines of America may inundate us with the precious metals, and the Government which has fixed its demand upon the land, may experience some diminution of its effective income from a fall in the value of money ; but it is also certain that, in a country where agriculture and commerce flourish, and where capital is allowed to accumulate, a more extensive medium of exchange becomes necessary, and a larger quantity of the precious metals is likely to be absorbed ; and, lastly, it may be safely affirmed that, if the population of a country be contented and rich, it never can be difficult for its rulers to draw from it those pecuniary resources which are necessary for the due administration of public affairs, and that although debts may be incurred during war to an inconvenient amount, a wise and just Government is likely to find a prosperous and well disposed people, able and willing to bear the burthen.

CHAPTER

CHAPTER IV.

FINANCIAL AND COMMERCIAL SITUATION OF
THE EAST-INDIA COMPANY.

———◆——

AFTER the review which has been taken of the resources of the East-India Company abroad, I propose to combine the territorial with the commercial accounts, in order to obtain, as far as may be practicable, materials for forming a correct judgment with respect to the financial situation of the Company *generally.*

It is not easy to form an accurate estimate of the commercial concerns of the Company, because they are not required to submit to Parliament an account of their profits or loss, and there is no direct evidence from which we can deduce the exact result of their commercial transactions. The Court of Directors have, however, in their financial correspondence, lately published, acknowledged on various occasions the existence of a commercial profit, and in a note subjoined to the last statement of their commercial stock, it is expressly declared that "the sum of £4,754,900 " sterling has been advanced, or set apart, from
" the

" the surplus commercial profits in England,
" towards the liquidation of Indian territorial
" debt."

It is true that the Company do not estimate their gains or loss with that degree of precision which a private merchant would consider necessary. They are their own insurers ; and as the casualties at sea occur very irregularly, the charge under this head is never determinate or equally distributed. Nor is interest charged on the exact amount of the capital* employed in the trade, including the cost of factories, warehouses, and other buildings. Moreover, until the late separation of the commercial and political accounts, the Customs in India, the salaries of the Boards of Trade, and other commercial establishments, were not charged on the Investment ; and there are still, I have reason to believe, various outlays incidental to the trade, which do not constitute a regular commercial charge : for example, the advances made to the manufacturers are, sometimes, irrecoverable ; and although the amount, after a time, is perhaps transferred to the account of " dead stock," as a desperate balance, the loss never appears

* The dividends on the Company's stock, and the interest on the bond debt, are charged in the commercial account; but their amount is scarcely equal to an interest of five per cent. per annum on the capital employed in the trade, including the " Dead Stock," and the Company pay in India, at the rate of six per cent. per annum.

appears as a direct charge upon the trade. In particular seasons, the loss occasioned by bad balances is very considerable, and this happens more especially in the instance of the silk investment; for as the rearing of the silk-worm is liable to be affected by different natural causes, a failure not unfrequently takes place; and whenever this occurs, the Company are the principal sufferers.

Without, however, enlarging on these and other circumstances, which make it impossible for me to ascertain with perfect precision the extent of the Company's commercial losses or gains, I shall proceed to examine those documents which may enable us to arrive, by an approximation, at the pecuniary results of their trade.

It is evident that, if we can obtain satisfactory evidence of the Company's situation at two given periods, at some distance from each other, a comparison between them will furnish a strong presumption with respect to the intervening events. If we can shew that the Company are richer at the present period than they were nine or ten years ago, the inference necessarily is, that they have realized a profit in the intermediate term. If they have become poorer, they must, of course, have sustained a loss.

Now, the statement of the Company's finances, which was submitted to Parliament soon after the renewal of their present charter, is very circumstantial,

stantial, and contains a full, and apparently a fair, exposition of their debts and assets, territorial and commercial, both abroad and at home, in the year 1815. The account for India is made up to the 30th of April, 1814 ; the home account is brought down to the 30th of April, 1815 ; but although it would, perhaps, have been more satisfactory if the two accounts had been made up to the same period, I am unwilling to destroy the identity of the statement, by introducing corrections* of my own, and I shall accordingly adhere to the official documents, preserving the same difference of a year at the close, as at the commencement of the term, which has been taken for the purposes of comparison.

The following abstract will shew the state of the commercial concern in 1814 and 1815, abroad and at home, respectively :

Commercial assets in India, on the 30th of April, 1814	£ 4,525,394
Ditto at home, ditto 1815	18,261,640
Total commercial assets	£22,787,034
Carry over.........	£22,787,034

* The net commercial assets in *India* in 1815, fell short of the amount in 1814, in the sum of £865,201, as follow :

Assets in 1815, after deducting debts	£3,332,340
Ditto, 1814, ditto	4,197,541
Less in 1815.........	£ 865,201

	Brought over.........	£22,787,034

Deduct
Commercial debt in India, on
   the 30th of April, 1814... £ 327,853
Ditto at home, ditto 1815...   2,156,417
                       2,484,270

           Commercial assets £20,302,764
Deduct, also,
Amount of bond debt at home, 30th of
   April, 1815   4,487,170

Net commercial balance in favour do.   £15,815,594

In this account the value of the India house and
other buildings and dead-stock is stated at the
sum of £1,143,000; and although the property
may not be saleable for this amount, it does not
appear to be an exaggerated valuation. Credit
is also taken for advances made in England, in
1814-15, on account of the territory, to the amount
of £2,304,626; and as it is to be presumed that
the statement is correct, I shall only observe that
the political charge in that year (£1,844,735) appears to have been on a much larger scale than it
is represented to have been at a later period.

I shall now proceed to contrast this state of the
commercial concern at the commencement of the
present charter with the results which the Indian
accounts of 1822, and the home accounts of 1823,
severally exhibit. I could bring down the statement

ment a year later, by making use of the manuscript accounts which were laid before the General Court of Proprietors on the 22d of December last; but as they have not yet been printed, and as the result of the comparison would not be materially different, I prefer to adhere to those public documents which can, if necessary, be referred to for the purpose of authenticating my statements.

Commercial assets in India, on the 30th of
    April, 1822 .... £ 3,085,724
    Ditto at home, ditto 1823.............. 23,792,441

               Total commercial assets £26,878,165
Deduct
  Commercial debt in India, on
    the 30th of April, 1822... £ 104,769
  Ditto at home, ditto 1823... 2,147,538
                      2,252,307

           Commercial assets £24,625,858
Deduct, also,
  Amount of bond debt at home, 30th of
    April, 1823........................ 3,937,729

  Commercial balance in favour do...... £20,688,129

This account, however, requires some adjustment, as it appears from the notes subjoined to the printed statements, that advances had been made in India on the commercial account in 1821-22

2 B   and

and 1822-23, to the amount of £4,600,000, which should properly be deducted from the commercial assets. On the other hand, it appears, that funds have been advanced from " the surplus commer-" cial profits" towards the liquidation of the territorial debt, between the 1st of May 1814, and the 1st of May 1823, to the amount of £3,358,060; and on the present occasion, where the object is to ascertain the extent of the commercial profit, this sum should be added to the commercial assets, as constituting a loan, or advance, made to the territorial department.

Commercial assets as above...............	£20,688,129
Deduct	
Territorial advances in India.........	4,600,000
	16,088,129
Add	
Advance on account of territorial debt from Commercial profit	3,358,060
Commercial balance in favour, in 1822-23	£19,446,189
Ditto do. do. in 1814-15	15,815,594
Increase of commercial assets	*£3,630,595

If

* This sum corresponds very nearly with the amount stated to have been advanced from the surplus of commercial profit to the territorial department, or £3,358,060.

If this estimate be correct, it would appear that a profit has been realized on the Company's commerce, in the course of eight years, to the amount of £3,630,595, or, on an average, at the rate of £453,824 per annum.

If the account were brought down to the 30th of April last, the result would not be quite so favourable, as there seems to have been a *decrease* in the commercial assets in the course of 1823-24;*

but

* Commercial assets abroad on the 30th of April, 1823		£ 1,938,541
Ditto at home, ditto 1824............................		22,746,469
Total assets		£24,685,010
Deduct		
Commercial debt abroad, 30th of April, 1823.......................	£ 537,487	
Ditto at home, ditto 1824	3,335,369	
Total debts.................		3,872,856
Net assets		£20,812,154
Deduct		
Advance in India from territory, for Commercial purposes, in 1823--24................................		2,450,000
		£18,362,154
Add		
Advance from the "surplus commercial profit," for the liquidation of territorial debt..............		4,754,902
		£23,117,056
Carry over......		£23,117,056

but I still think, upon the whole, that we may, with safety, estimate the average profit on the Company's trade at the sum of £450,000 per annum.

At this rate of profit an addition would be made to the commercial assets of £4,950,000 in the course of the next eleven years; and the Company at the expiration of the present charter in 1834, would remain possessed of a commercial capital to the amount of £24,500,000 sterling, after discharging the whole of the bond debt in this country.

This is the fund upon which the proprietors of India stock have a fair and legitimate claim for their indemnification; and it is quite clear, that, if the charter should not be renewed in 1834, they must be considered to be entitled to *a division of the commercial capital,* which ought to be quite sufficient

Brought over......	£23,117,056
Deduct	
Amount of bond debt, 30th of April, 1824	3,937,654
Commercial balance in favour of ditto ...	£19,179,402

The decrease appears to have arisen chiefly from the following commercial losses, viz. : —

Cargo of the Prince Regent, lost at sea.....................	£123,000
Value of woollens, &c. consumed by fire at Canton...	316,000
Bad balances written off and transferred to dead stock	200,000
	£639,000

sufficient to secure to them the value of their stock at its present price (290 per 100), after making ample allowance for the loss likely to be sustained on the sale of the India house and other immoveable property.

It should be observed, however, that in the commercial assets is included the sum set apart from the " surplus commercial profits," and appropriated to the liquidation of the territorial debt ; and if this advance, amounting, according to the latest statement, to £4,754,000,* should not ultimately be reclaimable from the territory, a corresponding deduction must be made from the amount of commercial capital.   Whether it was intended by the act of the 53d Geo. III. sec. 57, ch. 155, that the alienation of commercial profits, by their application to the fourth head of appropriation, should be *final,* or otherwise, is a question which I am not competent to decide ; but if the existing charter should not be renewed, it is to be presumed that the arrangement to be made with the proprietors of India stock, will proceed upon the principle that

---

* There may appear to be a contradiction in admitting a profit to this amount (£4,754,000) when I estimate the whole commercial profit realized in the course of eight years at only £3,630,595; but the former sum probably included profit realized in 1813-14, and indeed we find that the sum of £2,304,626, is stated to have been advanced to the Territory, from the Surplus of commercial Profits, prior to the 20th April, 1815.   A profit may also have been credited in 1823-24, although it does not appear to me that any was realized, after deducting the losses enumerated in a former note.

that they are entitled to any fund which can fairly be shewn to have arisen out of their commercial dealings.

It is also proper to explain, that, when the territorial and commercial accounts, were, for the first time separated in 1813-14, it had not been determined whether the bond debt in England appertained to the territory, or the commerce; but as the interest of that debt has been regularly paid from the commercial funds of the Company, it is to be inferred (although no adjustment appears yet to have taken place) that the whole of that debt is now considered to be chargeable to the commerce. In appropriating, then, the future commercial profits to the discharge of debt, it will be the interest of the proprietors of India stock that these bonds should be paid off in preference; and as the Court of Directors, with the sanction of the board of commissioners, may exercise a discretion, under the 57tn clause of the act already referred to, with respect to the selection of the debt to be *first* discharged, they will, no doubt, be attentive to the interests of the proprietors, as far as these interests can be consulted without prejudice to objects of higher consideration. Indeed, the honourable Court cannot be reproached with inattention to the commercial interests of the Company, real or supposed. On the contrary, a very narrow commercial spirit was known to prevail at a former period in their councils; and it is even now more than suspected that the feelings of the merchant sometimes
times

times prevail over the views of the statesman, and that the honourable Court have not yet so completely entered into their political character, as in all cases to assume with dignity the station, and to practise with constancy the duties, of legislators and sovereigns.

In estimating, as I have done, the future profits on the Company's trade, on the same scale as their past gains, or nearly half a million sterling per annum, it may be objected that their commerce is very much reduced, that their exports to India and China have been diminished, and that their home sales have of late fallen off in a still greater degree. The facts are certainly true but it does not follow that the inference drawn from them, is necessarily correct.

The exports to India and China, never, I believe, produced a profit *generally*, or for a continuance. The trade was resorted to, and persevered in, upon a variety of mixed considerations, partly, to supply a remittance to the East, where, until lately, we required funds for the purchase of return cargoes; partly, to supply the Chinese and our Indian subjects with articles which they could not obtain through other channels while the exclusive trade was vested in the Company; partly, to occupy tonnage, which would otherwise have been unproductive; but *chiefly* to benefit the manufacturing and other interests of this country, by

by introducing and circulating our Fabrics
and the produce of our mines throughout the
wide regions of Asia which were accessible to our
enterprize.

But as the Company no longer require a remittance *to* India, and as the trade to that country
has been thrown open to the British merchant,
who is not likely to be backward in supplying all
the demands of the foreign market, the Company have acted prudently and judiciously in circumscribing their* exports; and it is to be hoped

---

* The consignments to India, have rarely been attended with advantage. The Out-turns of those to China, from England and India,
have fluctuated greatly, especially in the instance of Cotton. A profit
of above 50 per cent. has sometimes been realized by the Company, on
this article; but on the other hand, severe losses have occasionally
been sustained on it and other articles (Long Ells, &c.). The following may be taken as a specimen (although I hope an unfavourable one)
of the result of the consignments to China.

In 1815-16, there was a *Loss* on the Woollens and
Metals sold, of about.. 16½ per cent.
In 1816-17, ...do.................do..................... 10¼ do.
1817-18, ...do.................do..................... 3¼ do.
1818-19, there was a *Profit* of about .... 8 do.
In 1815-16, the Cotton consigned from India, produced the following
rates of profit, *viz.*
That from Bombay,.. 56¼ per cent.
Do....do...Bengal .... 39¼ do.
Do....do...Madras .... 7¾ do.
The total supply to China, in that year, from England and India,
amounting to Taels 6,813,204, was attended with a loss of Taels
310,529, or about 4½ per cent. It may be doubted, however, whether
all the charges incidental to the trade (interest, insurance, &c. &c.),
are very accurately computed.

they will not hereafter recur to the practice of en-
gaging in a trade, promising only to be attended
with loss. I find the produce of their sales of
British goods in India in the last five years to have
been as follows :—*viz.*

In 1817-18	....	£605,706 sterling.
1818-19	....	727,945
1819-20	....	623,918
1820 21	....	513,404
1821-22	....	677,423

With respect to China, the case is somewhat
different, because that country is not directly open
to the enterprize of the British merchant ; and
while the Company retain the right to the exclusive trade, it is certainly incumbent upon them,
either to supply the China market themselves, as
far as this can be done with the prospect of advantage, or to allow others to supply it, to the full
extent of its demand for the produce of our mines
and of our manufacturing industry.

It has long been matter of doubt whether the
Company's trade from India has been attended
with a profit ; but since the late improvements in
the manufacture of British cottons, it has become
apparent that one great branch of that trade must
soon cease altogether. The human hand cannot
contend against the power of machinery ; and although some of the finer fabrics of India have never
been excelled, and its cotton manufactures gene-

2 c   rally

rally are more durable than those which are produced by machinery, the latter, by their superior cheapness, must ultimately command a preference. The Company, with a laudable desire to support their distressed manufacturers, and to preserve a beautiful and valuable fabric, have struggled to uphold a declining trade ;* and the British Legislature ought, upon every principle of justice, to second their efforts by† lowering the duties on the importation of Indian calicoes into this country, and its dependencies, to the rates which British calicoes pay on their introduction into India ; but even with this concession in their favour, there are very few articles which could maintain a successful competition with our home-manufactures in any of the markets of consumption.

The following statement will shew the amount of the investments purchased by the Company in India,

* Whether this struggle can be justified by the principles of *political economy*, may be fairly questioned; but the wish to support theirstarving manufacturers was natural and praiseworthy; and the exertions of a respectable Director (Mr. Bebb) to save them from ruin, were characteristic of that just and upright man.

† Since these pages have been in the press, the exorbitant duties on Indian Cotton Goods, have been reduced, and I hail this fair commencement of a wise and just policy; but much remains to be done to place the commerce of India upon a proper footing. The present concession is valuable, as a pledge that more will be done hereafter : the immediate boon is not very great, as I fear that Indian Calicoes cannot be imported even at the reduced duty of ten per cent ad valorem.

India, for consignment to this country, in the last
ten years :—*viz.*

In 1812-13	£2,017,092
1813 14	1,686,580
1814-15	1,136,525
1815-16	1,234,096
1816-17	1,162,263
1817-18	1,553,733
1818-19	1,166,946
1819-20	1,477,820
1820-21	1,534,917
1821-22	1,266,046

In some instances the purchases may be said to
have been *forced,* there existing an urgent necessity at the time for the Company to obtain a remittance, on whatever terms, to enable them to provide for the payment of bills drawn from India in
discharge of the principal and interest of the territorial debt. Large remittances in bullion were
also made at different times for the same purpose;
and it is to be apprehended that they may again
be necessary, in the ensuing year, to enable
the Court of Directors to provide for the payment
of the septennial loan of 1818, and of the bills which
will have been drawn by the supreme government
on the 30th of September last in satisfaction of a
portion of the loan of 1811. The honourable
Court very properly granted the option of a re-
2 c 2 mittance

mittance to the public creditors in this country, whose notes were to be paid off; and the accommodation is not likely to be attended with loss to the Company at the exchange fixed for the bills (*viz.* 2*s.* the Sicca rupee). Indeed, if there be any thing to regret, it is that more liberal terms were not granted to these creditors, who have suffered severely under the operation of our financial arrangements.

The aggregate produce of the Company's sales in England, in the last three years, will shew a very great falling off when compared with the amount sales in the first two years of the present charter :—*viz.*

Amount of sales in 1813-14	£8,452,828
1814-15	7,359,978
Sales in 1821-22	5,262,348
1822-23	5,566,564
1823-24	5,260,680

The sales, however, in 1813-14 and 1814-15, were unusually large, owing probably in a great degree to the opening of the continental markets on the return of peace ; and, although they are now on a reduced scale, yet, as by far the larger portion of the amount is the produce of the China trade, which alone is supposed to have yielded a regular profit, I see no reason to apprehend that the commercial gain is less, at the present moment,

ment, than it was when the importations of the Company were much more extensive.

It has been supposed that the Company derive an inordinate profit from their trade in tea, and a clamour has been raised against them on the ground that the people of this country are heavily taxed to administer to the avarice of a body of insatiate monopolists. It may be useful then to examine the facts of the case, in order to ascertain how far there is a foundation for the complaint.

If the British consumer pay, on an average, six shillings per pound for his tea, let it be remembered that a moiety of this sum (or three shillings) goes into the public exchequer. The government duty does not amount, it is true, to quite a moiety of the cost to the consumer, it being levied on the *wholesale* prices; but the difference is not material, and my computation of the Company's profit will, of course, be founded upon the wholesale prices.

Now, with respect to this first element in the price of tea, the question to be decided is, *whether the tax on that article be judicious, or otherwise.* The duty is, no doubt, very high, and excessive duties on this, or any other article of consumption, have a tendency to encourage smuggling and to produce adulteration, as well as to check consumption. It was on this ground that the late

Mr.

Mr. Pitt lowered the duties on tea, and substituted a commutation tax; but they have again been raised, and very recently too; and we are bound, therefore, to presume that the contribution of near four millions per annum, which is levied from the consumers of tea, is required for national objects, and that it cannot be otherwise obtained by any better expedient. I do not mean to affirm that the tax on tea is the best of all possible taxes; but, I do maintain, that a tax which can be avoided, and which does not press heavily on the lower orders, is less objectionable than the tax on coals, or the tax on light and air, and other objects, the use of which cannot be dispensed with by any class of the people, without a deprivation of comfort, and possible injury to health. For the present, then, it must be admitted, that nearly half the price paid by the consumers of tea finds its way to the public exchequer for national purposes, and does not enter the coffers of the East India Company.

The second element in the price of this article is *the interest on the capital employed*; and, we must not suppose that it is chargeable only on the amount of the annual sale, or four millions: the capital on which the charge of interest is incurred, is probably not less than ten millions, consisting, as it does, of the value of tea held in store in this country and in China,

as

as well as the cost of the tea in transitu, and of the export cargoes, which are intended as a remittance for the purchase of the article, together with the value of the buildings, warehouses, and other apparatus required for the trade. An interest at the rate of 4 per cent. on this capital, would amount to the sum of £400,000 ;* and, in point of fact, the commercial account is charged annually under this head, in the shape of dividends to the proprietors and interest on the bond debt, to the amount of about £780,000, the greater part of which is properly a charge on the tea investment.

It may be alleged, that the private merchant would carry on the trade with a much smaller capital,

---

* The Company charge the tea of 1822-23 with interest to the amount of £237,899 only ; but this is much below the charge actually incurred. I do not know the data assumed for the calculation ; but, it would be quite an error to suppose, that interest is incurred only on the amount sales of one year. I should calculate it on the following capital, viz. :—

Prime cost of tea brought to sale annually	£2,000,000
Ditto of one year's consumption in store	2,000,000
Ditto ditto in transitu from China.........	2,000,000
Value of outward cargoes and remittances from India for the purchase of tea.................................	2,000,000
Advances to merchants, cash and stock at Canton, &c.	1,000,000
Cash and stock in England.................................	1,000,000
	£10,000,000

capital, since his returns would be *annual,* by reason of his employing smaller ships, calculated to perform the voyage out and home within the year. This is partly true; but, under any circumstances, the capital employed must far exceed the amount of the annual sale. A stock of tea must always be held in reserve, into whatever hands the trade might devolve; and upon the whole capital employed, the charge of interest is necessarily incurred. Were no such stock maintained, not only would the public be exposed to inconvenience from a failure in the accustomed supply, but the prices would be liable to sudden and violent fluctuations; and the consumer would often have to pay, in the advance of price, much more than he would save in consequence of a smaller amount of interest entering into the original cost of the article. Warehouses, too, and all the other appurtenances of trade, would be required, whether the commerce were carried on by the Company, or by private individuals.

The third element in the price of tea is the charge of *freight and demurrage,* which, on the quantity annually consumed in England, may be stated at £450,000, at the rate at present paid by the Company for their China tonnage. In this estimate it is assumed, that the return cargo is properly chargeable with the *whole* freight, since the exports from hence, as well as the exports

ports of cotton, sandal wood, and other articles from the Presidencies of India, are understood to produce no more than a saving remittance.*

It may here, also, be objected, that the private
merchant, by employing a different class of ships,
would be able to procure tonnage on much
cheaper terms.† This is unquestionably true;
but a preference has been given to the ships at
present employed, on the ground that they are
peculiarly well adapted to the trade. They are
certainly equipped and appointed in the completest manner : they are navigated by experienced officers ; are capable of defence in time of
war ; and, although they perform only one voyage
in two years, which necessarily renders the freight
more expensive, it is to be presumed that they
would not command a preference, if those in
whom the decision of the question has been vested, were not satisfied that there are circumstances
in their favour, sufficient to outweigh the objections,

---

* See a former note on the subject.

† The freight paid by the Company last year, for their China
cargoes, averaged £21 : 11s. 1d. per ton. Smaller ships which should
perform the voyage within the year, could afford to sail at £12 per
ton, out and home ; but the port charges at Canton are somewhat
higher, I believe, in proportion, on smaller ships. The rate of insurance, or value of the risk, might also be somewhat higher ; but the
difference would not be material in either of these items.

jections, originating in the higher charge of freight.

Another item connected with the foregoing, is the charge for *insurance,* or the value of the risk (the Company being their own insurers); but this is of small account, for in the instance of such superior ships as the larger class of Indiamen, sailing as they do from China almost invariably at the favourable season, and bearing a light buoyant cargo, the sea risk on the homeward voyage is very inconsiderable. It does not probably exceed $2\frac{1}{2}$ per cent., or about £50,000, on the value of the tea annually imported ; and I find it stated accordingly in the Company's accounts of 1822-23 at £59,528, say £60,000.

The commercial disbursements of the Company at Canton amount to about £50,000 per annum, and the charges of merchandize in this country to £412,000. The whole of the former, and a large portion of the latter, must be placed to the account of the tea investment, the only part of the trade which can bear the charge; and I should be disposed to state the aggregate at not less than £325,000, or about 9 per cent. on the annual sales. It is stated at only £307,006,* in

* Charges in China.. 50,649
    Do. in England...176,841
Commission and allowances to supra-cargoes, &c........... 79,516

£.307,006

the

the printed accounts of 1822-23; but this sum appears to me to be below the proportion properly chargeable to the tea investment.

It may be urged that, if the trade were in private hands, it would be managed in a more economical way; but, the private merchant would have occasion to employ an agent in China, to whom he must pay a Commission* on his sales and purchases; and, if the commerce were distributed among fifty or an hundred merchants, as it probably would be, on the trade being opened, the aggregate of their separate establishments (counting-houses, clerks, &c. &c.) would not probably fall short of the expense at present incurred by the Company.

Into the *retail* price paid by the consumer, another ingredient necessarily enters, namely: the profit of the broker, wholesale merchant, and retail trader, and all the expenses incurred by these parties, respectively, in supplying the consumption from the time that the tea leaves the Company's warehouse. But, without attempting to estimate this item, I shall proceed to recapitulate

* A commission of 2 per cent is divided among the Company's supra-cargoes and servants at Canton; and, the usual rate of commission, on purchases and sales in India and China, is, I believe, 2¼ per cent. There would, consequently, be no saving in this item by the private merchant; nor does it appear to me probable, that his charges of merchandize, in the aggregate, would fall short of the amount incurred by the Company.

2 D 2

late the elements which compose the *wholesale* price of the article;

1st Government duty of 100 per cent...	£3,725,000
2d Prime cost of the tea in China	1,925,000
3d Interest on capital employed at 4 per cent per annum......................	400,000
4th Freight and demurrage	450,000
5th Insurance..........................	*60,000
6th Charges of merchandize in China and England.......................	325,000
Government duty, and cost and charges	£6,885,000
Gross amount sales on an average of eleven years, including duty	7,450,000
Estimated profit annually	£565,000

equal to about 15 per cent. on the amount sales, exclusive of duty, or to about $5\frac{1}{2}$ per cent. on the capital employed, after defraying the charge of interest. This rate of profit would not be considered very exorbitant, or unreasonable, if it were drawn by the private merchant as the remuneration of his personal labour; and, it is, as nearly as I can estimate it, *the sum total of the contribution*

† I ought, perhaps, to charge insurance also on the outward cargo, since it in reality constitutes the purchase money of the tea investment. I have adopted this principle in charging the tea with the whole freight of the tonnage which it occupies; but the outward cargo ought, one year with another, to furnish a saving remittance after defraying charges, freight excepted.

contribution levied by the East India Company on the British consumer of tea.

The annual profit on the tea investment, deduced as above-mentioned, amounts to £565,000; and, as this sum exceeds the average profit which I have supposed to be realized on the *whole* trade (£450,000 per annum), it follows, either that the annual gain has been under-estimated by me, or that a part of the profit on the tea trade is absorbed in *losses* sustained on other branches of the Company's commerce. The *latter* supposition I take to be the more probable of the two.

Now, it may be urged that the rate of profit drawn by the Company, or about $5\frac{1}{2}$ per cent., exceeds the average profits of trade at the present period in this country; and that their monopoly consequently operates as a tax upon the consumer, to the extent at least of the excess. This may, or may not, be true; but, admitting the fact, in what manner are the profits of the Company appropriated? are they applied to increase the fortunes of individuals? to gratify the avarice of the proprietors of India stock? Certainly not. Those proprietors are restrained by law from dividing more than $10\frac{1}{2}$ per cent, on the *nominal* amount of their stock, or about $3\frac{1}{2}$ per cent, on the *real* value of the capital. The surplus commercial profits of the Company, have been appropriated to the discharge of a portion of the

the territorial debt ; which, sooner or later, must become a national concern. The territory is pledged for that debt ; and, although the security is ample, the incumbrance would have been much greater, if the debt had not been reduced, or kept within bounds, by the application of the commercial profits to its liquidation. That element, therefore, in the price of tea, which is composed of the Company's profit, may be regarded very much in the same light as the government duty of 100 per cent. *the tax being levied for public * purposes.*

If the people of Great Britain are desirous of drinking their tea on the same terms as the people of America, it is undoubtedly in their option to have it at 3s, or 2s. 6d. per pound, instead of 6s. or 5s. 6d. per pound, *after the very next session of Parliament.* They have imposed upon themselves the duty of 100 per cent., and it rests with them to take it off, whenever they please; but, before they resort to such a measure, it will certainly be proper for them to consider whether any better alternative presents itself; and whether, in repealing or reducing one tax, they might not find it necessary to have recourse

* Unless, indeed, the whole of the profits so appropriated, should hereafter be refunded to the proprietors of India Stock, who have certainly a claim upon this fund.

recourse to a substitute of a still more objectionable character.

I am, at the same time, far from meaning to contend that the East India Company are not bound to attend to the interests, and to consult the convenience and comfort of the British consumer. Their monopoly was granted with a view to great national objects; and, in order to render the prices of their teas more moderate, they ought, I think, by degrees to increase their annual sales, and to endeavour to draw the same profits, or even a reduced profit (if the present rate be unreasonably high), upon a more extended consumption of the article. I have observed with regret, that the annual purchases in China, as well as the sales in this country, have been nearly stationary* of late years; but, from the increase which appears to have taken place in the sales of the last year, it is intended, I hope, gradually

			lbs.	sterling.
* Purchases of tea in China in		1819-20	28,476,231	£1,877,402
Ditto	ditto	1820-21	28,545,960	1,896,476
Ditto	ditto	1821-22	25,746,439	1,852,715
Ditto	ditto	1822-23	27.478,813	1,924,738

Sales in England,		lbs.
1820	about	26,100,000
1821	...	27,600,000
1822	...	27,800,000
1823	...	27,700,000
1824	...	28,300,000

gradually to extend them. Tea is not an article, like opium, where it is desirable to levy the largest revenue upon the smallest quantity. The consumption of the latter it may be proper to check, as injurious to health and morals. The consumption of tea, on the contrary, ought perhaps to be encouraged, as being conducive to comfort, and as tending to exclude the use of a less harmless beverage.

The Court of Directors have lately adopted a judicious arrangement for supplying our American colonies with tea, by a direct importation from China; and it is only surprising, that a measure so well calculated to accommodate the colonial consumer, to encourage our own shipping, and to put an end to a contraband trade from the United States, should not have been resorted to at an earlier period.

I have now given a hasty, and, I fear, an imperfect sketch of the commercial affairs of the East-India Company, and it is, I am aware, much too concise to satisfy those who are accustomed to look minutely into a subject. He, however, who undertakes to treat of Indian topics, and to draw attention to the state of our remote possessions in the East,* sees presented to him the horns

of

* The affairs of India seem to attract more attention at present on the continent than they do in this country, deeply as we are interested in them. M. de Sismondi has followed closely on the footsteps of

of a dilemma : if he enter much into detail, he commands few readers ; if he condense his matter, there is reason to apprehend that he will not satisfy the understanding of those to whom he addresses himself. With this difficulty before me, I have confined myself to such a statement as appeared to me likely to convey some general and useful information, without being absolutely repulsive by the extent and complicacy of the details.

I shall now proceed to combine the territorial with the commercial accounts, and to place in one view the general results at which we have arrived.

It has been shewn that, during a season of peace, a surplus territorial revenue is likely to be realized in India to the extent of two millions sterling per annum, after defraying all local charges, and providing for the interest of the territorial debt.

2dly. That this surplus is liable to an annual deduction, to the amount of one million and a half, on account of territorial and political disbursements

M. Say, vide "La Revue Encyclopédique" for December, pages 635 ad 656. These writers do not appear to have drawn their information always from the latest or most authentic sources; but we should not disregard the remarks of intelligent spectators, who sometimes see the game better than the players. I cannot admit either M. de Sismondi's premises or deductions on several important points; but as the questions which he notices are much too weighty to be disposed of in a summary way, I shall not undertake to discuss them in this place.

ments made in this country, leaving a net surplus revenue, derivable from our Eastern possessions, of five hundred thousand pounds per annum.

3dly. That the debt of India, bearing interest, amounted, on the 30th of April 1822, to the sum of £31,623,780 sterling, entailing an annual charge of £1,896,524; and the net territorial debt, abroad and at home, after deducting assets, to the sum of £16,386,953.

4thly. That the commercial *assets,* and *credits* abroad and at home, after deducting the bond debt and other commercial debts, amounted, in 1823, 24, to the sum of *£14,424,500, constituting a fund, properly belonging to the proprietors of India stock for the replacement of their capital.†

5thly. That a profit is drawn from the Company's trade, after providing for the dividends to the proprietors and the interest of the bond debt, and after defraying all the expenses of their establishment, abroad and at home, to the estimated amount of £450,000 per annum.

6thly. That the net income of the Company, terri-

* Or above nineteen millions, if the accounts between the commerce and the territory be adjusted upon the basis that the former can reclaim the amount of commercial profits, which has been applied to the liquidation of territorial debt.—See Appendix B.

† This capital is stated in the Company's accounts at £7,780,000, which I presume to be the sum actually received into the treasury from the proprietors. It may now be considered worth between £17,000,000 and £18,000,000.

territorial and commercial, during a period of peace, may accordingly be assumed at about one million sterling per annum, which is applicable to the gradual liquidation of debt, or to the augmentation of their commercial capital.

7thly. That since the commencement of the present charter, an improvement has taken place in the financial situation of the Company, *territorial* and *commercial, abroad* and *at home,* to the extent of near three millions sterling,* notwithstanding our having been engaged intermediately in several expensive wars.

This exposition of the Company's finances must certainly be regarded as highly favourable and satisfactory, and nothing but the intervention of an unfortunate war, which the authorities in this country could neither foresee nor prevent, was likely to have checked the prosperous course of their affairs.

The proprietors of India stock will perceive from this summary that they possess security for their capital, if the charter of the Company should be withdrawn. In that case, they would either

---

* Vide Appendix B. Net Deficiency in 1814-15 ... £2,611,311
            Net Surplus in 1823-24   187,807

            Amelioration £2,799,118

either be entitled to a division of the commercial assets ; or their present dividends must be continued to them as perpetual annuities, should the government think proper to dispose otherwise of those assets. In common justice, their claims to be recognized, in one or other character, either as the proprietors of the commercial capital, or as fixed annuitants, cannot well be disputed ; and while there are funds upon which they have so just a claim, no plea could be urged for placing them in a worse condition than that of other corporate bodies, who, after the expiration of the term for which they have been associated, are allowed to divide their profits and their capital.

Even if the sum which has been taken from the " surplus commercial profits" (£4,754,900), for the liquidation of the political debt, should not be restored, and the commerce should be charged with the home bond debt (£3,937,000), the commercial capital at the expiration of the charter in 1834, may still be expected to amount, at the computed rate of profit, to a sum sufficient to indemnify the proprietors of East India stock for their capital at its present valuation.

The creditors abroad have the security of a territory, yielding a revenue of twenty-two millions sterling per annum, and a net surplus of half a million ; and whenever the administration of that territory shall be assumed by the Crown, it is

to

to be presumed that their interests and the security of their property, will be effectually provided for.

Whether the existing system for the administration of the territory and for regulating the trade, be the best which can be devised, and be essentially calculated to produce the greatest attainable good, both to India and to the mother country, is a question which will come before the British public at no distant period. It is one of incalculable importance, both as it affects the interests of Great Britain and the well-being of the vast population which has been subjected to her dominion ; and whenever the proper season shall arrive, it will, I trust, be examined with unprejudiced feelings, and be disposed of, after mature consideration, upon those sound and just views of policy, which ought to decide all questions of great national concern. I have confined myself as much as possible to the professional subject which I undertook to discuss, and I am unwilling to pass the bounds which I have prescribed to myself; but without intending to encroach upon the province of the statesman, it is natural to ask, *with views merely financial,* how has a revenue of twenty-two millions per annum been acquired by us ? Under what wise and salutary institutions has it been preserved ? And what assurance

surance have we of its future prosperity and permanency?

The government abroad has, in general, been
ably and successfully administered,* and the great
body of our native subjects enjoy a degree of protection and security in their persons and property,
unknown to the subjects of the Hindoo and Mahomedan states around us. The constitution of
that government is, I think, well suited to the peculiar circumstances of our situation, the character of our dominion, and the disposition and habits
of the people with whom we are associated, either
in our domestic or external relations. This government is not a pure despotism, as has been alleged. It is a government of *law* and *responsibility*,
acting under numerous and salutary checks. The
administrators of that government exercise a delegated power; they are accountable agents, who
are

---

* I am not called upon to offer an opinion on the justice and necessity of our different wars, nor on the character of our proceedings towards our dependent allies, the most questionable branch of our administration in India. The philosopher, meditating on these events at
a distance from the scene of action, may, no doubt, find much to condemn and to lament; but after the recent exposure of the condition of the Hyderabad territory, it cannot be doubted that the public
authorities will see the necessity of rescuing the national character
from reproach by placing our connection with the dependent states
on a less objectionable footing.

are amenable to the courts of law in England, to the authority of the Court of Directors, the Court of Proprietors, the Commissioners for Indian Affairs, the two Houses of Parliament, the Crown, and the British Public. To render this control efficient, they are required *to record their most minute transactions,* and they do record, regularly and faithfully, every public act, with a scrupulous exactness, unprecedented in any other country. They are also required, in their legislative capacity, to record, upon the face of every law, the special reasons for the enactment; and if these laws are neglected and thrown upon the shelf on their arrival in England, the defect lies in the *practice* and not in the *theory.*

Moreover, the government, for all official acts, and the public officers, in their individual capacity, are subject to the jurisdiction of the King's courts, established at the three presidencies, as well as to the jurisdiction of the courts of Adawlut, established throughout our provinces, and acting under the authority of written laws, recognised and sanctioned by the British legislature.

The government of India has, it is true, been entrusted with vast powers; and they are necessary, I think, for the preservation of our dominion ; but these powers are exercised by agents, who are removeable at pleasure; and if they be grossly abused, and the abuse be not visited with the
penalties

penalties justly incurred ; if at any time acts of violence and injustice obtain unmerited impunity, it is not that responsibility does not *attach*, but that it has not been duly *enforced*.

The selection of the supreme Governors of India, for more than half a century, has been either very judicious, or very fortunate ; and there has been this remarkable felicity attending it, that the individuals seem to have been peculiarly suited to the particular times and circumstances in which they happen to have been placed. They could not, perhaps, in any one instance, have changed places with advantage. The genius and enterprize of Lord Clive achieved the conquest of an empire. The fertile resources of Mr. Hastings' mind enabled him to preserve that empire under circumstances of extraordinary difficulty. Lord Cornwallis, eminent alike as a statesman and soldier, took charge of the government at a time when the elements of our power were beginning to assume consistency, but required to be moulded into form by a powerful hand ; and the natural rectitude and energy of his character disposed him to introduce wholesome reforms, and to establish a regular system of internal administration, founded upon principles of justice, and the views of a benevolent policy. Lord Teignmouth, possessing great knowledge and experience, followed in the footsteps of his illustrious predecessor ; and with
scrupulous

scrupulous good faith, gave effect to plans which,
as a member of Lord Cornwallis' government, he
had felt it his duty to oppose.* The great talents
of Lord Wellesley were called into action at a
momentous crisis. France, after overpowering
the continent of Europe by a great convulsive
movement, directed her ambitious views to the
East, and there found powerful allies in the Mahomedan state of Mysore, and in the French
commanders, who, at the head of large bodies of
organized troops in the service of the Nizam and
of Dowlut Rao Scindiah, were prepared to dispute with us our ascendancy in India. The mo-
ther-country was engaged in a struggle for existence, and we were left to our own resources and
exertions. Egypt was already occupied by the
French, as the first step in their adventurous career; but the talents of Lord Wellesley were equal
to the emergency, and surmounted it ; and the
novel spectacle was exhibited in this administration of an Indian army co-operating with British
troops on the banks of the Nile. When, after sus-
taining successive conflicts, our strength was im-
paired, and repose became necessary to recruit our
exhausted resources, the wisdom and prudence
and

* I allude merely to the question of the " Permanent Settlement."
The general maxims of Lord Teignmouth's government corresponded,
I believe, with those which Lord Cornwallis had acted upon.

and pacific policy of Sir George Barlow and the
Earl of Minto, restored the state to all its pristine
vigour; while the conquest of Java and the French
islands sufficiently attests, that, on proper occasions, Lord Minto could display all the decision
and enterprize which usually give assurance of a
superior mind : and, finally, the military and political administration of the Marquess of Hastings,
full of energy and spirit, added new lustre to the
reputation of our arms, and gave a wider range to
British supremacy in the East.

But I may be told, that our success and the
merits of our rule are to be referred to the personal
qualities of the rulers, rather than to the inherent
merits of our institutions. This must, in part, be
admitted ; and in what country does it not happen
that the well-being of the governed is to be referred mainly to the qualities of the governors?
It is true that there is this peculiarity in our situation in India : the rulers being foreigners, and as
such not identified with the people, they cannot
be displaced *by the people*, without the overthrow
of the sovereignty itself; whereas in countries in
which the governors and the governed have one
common origin, the rulers may be removed without destroying the constitution or system of government.

I fully admit that much depends upon the personal qualities of those who are selected to administer

nister our affairs in India. The government can never become a safe sinecure: it is a fatal mistake to suppose that our work in that country has been consummated, or ever can be consummated: it requires scarcely less talent to *preserve* than was necessary to *create*. Although our dominion has been extended to the utmost verge which could have been desired, although our power has been consolidated, and our name is respected and feared, we can never with safety relax in vigilant circumspection, or entrust our affairs to feeble hands. The transitory days of peace ought to be welcomed when they do arrive; but they ought never to be regarded as a season exempt from difficulty and danger. It cannot be concealed, and it ought not to be concealed, that the position in which the native states* of India are placed, is not a natural one, nor one of their own choice, which they submit to willingly. They are under a certain pressure, enforced by superior power. He who has

---

* The same may be said of some of our own once-powerful subjects and dependents. For instance, the Rajahs of Hàtras, Moorsàn, Pritchetghur, Lundoura, &c., once feudatory chieftains, have been compressed into the condition of simple landholders. In fact, although I have thought it right to point out that we never can depend upon the continuance of peace (for even the resuscitation of the Pindarries would not greatly surprise me), I do not consider our external enemies as the chief source of danger to our power. *Our greatest danger*, in my opinion, *will always be from within.*

has seen (the illustration is homely, I own) a bale of cotton compressed into one-fourth of its natural dimensions, may form a notion of the sort of force which restrains them in their present situations. The mass seems inert; but there is an elastic force within, which is ready to expand : relax the cords, and it immediately manifests itself.

And the philanthropist may say, *cut* the cords, and let them be free and happy. But this is an operation which involves many serious contingencies; not merely the subversion of our own empire, but the introduction of absolute anarchy and misrule throughout a large portion of Asia. Who that has read in the pages of Sir John Malcolm the teeming record of massacres and pillage, would wish to see the population of the desolated region which he describes, committed once more to a Mahratta * plunderer, or an Affghan adventurer ? Who could see, without deep regret, the flourishing provinces of Bengal converted into a waste, the scene of bloodshed and disorder, of religious contention, unbridled violence, and lawless oppression? No ; the people of India are not prepared for self government ; they are not sufficiently advanced in knowledge ; they do not properly

* The administration of Ahilya Bhye throws a gleam of sunshine over Marhatta history, and Sir John has succeeded in giving a dramatic interest to the character of this princess; but the other side of the picture is only darkened by the contrast : it is an Oasis in the desert.

properly appreciate the advantages of political
morality; and they are unacquainted with those
great principles and maxims of political wisdom,
upon which all government ought to be founded.
Whatever may be our disqualifications as foreigners, we govern them better than they
could govern themselves; and our dominion, if
it avert no other evil than the sanguinary struggle
which is likely to take place whenever our authority may be withdrawn, must be regarded
as eminently calculated to promote the great
interests of humanity.

Of the administration at home, I have observed,
that it may claim the rare merit of having made
a judicious selection of functionaries to conduct
the public affairs abroad. This is doing much
for India ; since, in point of fact, the great business of government must be carried on abroad.
Measures relating to its internal administration
can seldom be *originated* here with advantage :
but still the system of administration at home
is very far from being matter of indifference.
Where the powers committed to the local authorities are so extensive, and the discretion so ample,
the means of controlling those authorities should be
proportionally strong and efficient.* If they are
commissioned

---

* The honourable Court of Directors well observe, " It is a self-
" evident proposition that in proportion to the extent of power

commissioned to make laws upon which the
welfare of millions may depend, we should see
that those laws are founded on principles of justice,
and are not inconsistent with those important
truths, which the reason and experience of an
enlightened age have established.

And may we fairly assume, that this great duty
has been adequately provided for? Are our institutions at home well adapted to the ends which
they are intended to accomplish? Those who
have seen the workings of the machinery, and who
are most friendly to the existing order of things,
will scarcely venture to pronounce that it is
perfect. The two administrative bodies are *con-
flicting* and not *concurring* authorities ; and their
collision is calculated to produce delay, incon-
gruities, and sometimes an absolute suspension
of the functions of government. The process by
which a decision on any important question is
arrived at, is so slow and embarrassed, that the
proper season of action may pass away before
a resolution can be carried into effect. He who
introduces a measure, is often obliged to leave
it to be executed by another; and, perhaps, by
the very individual by whom it had been opposed.

He

" vested in any individual, ought to be the strictness of responsibility
" for its due exercise and the checks upon its abuse."— See Letter to
Bengal, in Hyderabad Papers, page 390.

He who is indolent, timid, or wavering, allows
the machine to remain at rest, to be propelled
by a more adventurous successor. The mode of
distributing the business among the public functionaries may also admit of question, since it has
no reference to their respective qualifications and
previous habits; but, on the other hand, it is
contended that the experience which is obtained
in the course of passing through the different
committees, has been found of great advantage
to those who are ultimately called upon to
execute the high office of chairman. To this
consideration I am disposed to allow every degree
of weight ; and I am seldom inclined to oppose
mere speculative opinions to the safer deductions
which experience supplies : yet, admitting all
which is contended for, I still think that professional knowledge and peculiar attainments
might be brought to bear with better effect upon
the public service, under a modification of the
existing arrangement.

But the great defect in the system is the *total
absence of all responsibility.* By responsibility, I
do not mean merely the liability to penalties
imposed by the law : high public functionaries
can seldom be brought to punishment ; but, if
the individual *be identified with his acts,* an opera-
tive principle is supplied in the honest love of
fame, and in the dread of public odium. Public
censure,

censure, justly incurred, is one of the severest punishments to which a mind, not hardened and callous, can well be exposed.

The government of India, holding only a delegated trust, can be rendered strictly accountable to the superintending authorities at home, to the law, and to parliament ; and all its acts can be distinctly referred to the individuals by whom they have been committed : but the administrative authorities at home are so constituted, that responsibility, the best check and restraint upon the exercise of power, is no where found to attach to any beneficial purpose. When divided among numbers, responsibility is necessarily reduced to a fraction of small value ; but the practice of deciding public questions by the ballot is calculated to do away even the semblance of it. I am aware that the Directors are at liberty to record, within fourteen days, their dissent from any decision of a majority : but, although this privilege is calculated to answer a useful purpose, and would, if more frequently exercised, point to the authors of particular measures, by shewing *who have not been parties to them ;* yet it is rather intended to exonerate from responsibility than to fix it upon individuals : besides, the Court of Directors, in merely originating measures, cannot justly be held responsible for them, if those measures be altered and perhaps reversed by a

higher

higher authority—and that higher authority cannot justly be made responsible for the general
conduct of affairs, to which it cannot give the first
momentum, and over which it exerts only a
repressive control. The good sense and good
feeling of the two authorities, acting under a
strong sense of public duty, and interchanging
their respective opinions in the liberal spirit which
is habitual to men of high intellectual endowment,
may prevent collision, and may produce measures
distinguished for their wisdom and propriety; but
this, when it happens, is a contingent good, result-
ing from individual character, and we can have no
assurance of its continuance, when the powers of
government are exercised by irresponsible agents,
or when they are liable to be paralised or enfeebled
by the contentions of those agents.

If these defects were not susceptible of a remedy, it would be worse than useless to notice
them, and they have not been noticed in the spirit
of crimination ; but, every well-wisher of the
Company (without adverting to concerns of
higher interest) must be desirous of seeing its
administration so far improved as to be free from
all just reproach, and to become the object of
public esteem. To correct defects is the obvious
way to disarm adversaries, and to justify the
support of friends.

Whatever may be the imperfections of the
2 G   system,

system, it cannot justly be arraigned on the
ground that it has led to an improvident administration of the finances, the question which
more immediately concerns us at present. They
have, in general, been managed both abroad and
at home, with integrity, intelligence, and zeal.
Instances of profuse and even wasteful expenditure might be pointed out ; but they are not
numerous, and the instances of embezzlement
and corruption, which have come to light, have
not been more frequent ; and, far from being
screened, on discovery, by the public authorities
abroad or at home, the individuals have been visited with merited punishment, and have met with
no countenance or support from a service which
highly estimates the value of its public character.

Nor can it be alleged that public services have
been rewarded with too munificent a hand : on the
contrary, the Court of Directors have been reproached for unseasonable parsimony ; and, they
have not, perhaps, always recollected that, as they
have no civil honors to bestow, pecuniary rewards
and just commendation can alone mark their sense
of public merit.* The liberal remuneration of
eminent

* Let it be recollected that, while the Crown has with great propriety, justice, and policy established a graduated scale of honors to
be conferred as the reward of military service, the civil officers of the
Company, however eminent their merits and services, cannot look
forward

eminent services is quite consistent with the practice of a just economy, and may be vindicated
upon public principles ; but, the Court of Directors are the trustees of the public purse, and
in closing it against importunate claims they
can have no private feeling to gratify.

To conclude: When we reflect that an empire,
acquired by valour and skill, and preserved by
wisdom and prudence, has been governed in the
spirit of moderation and justice; that the countries
over which our sway extends, enjoy a state of
tranquillity and prosperity unknown in the neighbouring territory ; and that a revenue has been
created in this remote dependency, exceeding the
income of some of the most powerful states of
Europe, we must acknowledge that the system of
administration, whatever may be its theoretical
defects, must have its redeeming virtues, and
must have been regulated and superintended by
men of no ordinary capacity and merit.   And
whatever may be the fate of the East-India Company, at whatever period that body shall cease to
exist,

forward to any public distinction. This is, I think, a deficiency.
Fortune, no doubt, gives consideration in this country ; but, wealth
is not the paramount good with some men, and the civil servants of
the Company can seldom realize large fortunes by honourable means.
In no country are the minds of men more exercised, and in no
country can a government have stronger motives for exciting its
servants to honorable exertion.

exist, it may challenge comparison with any colonial administration, of which we have record in
any age or country ; while the pages of its history,
fertile in instances of political wisdom and military
skill, of gallant enterprize and splendid success,
will perpetuate the memory of a brilliant and
eventful career, not surpassed by the proudest
achievements of Gallic ambition, or the noblest
triumphs of Roman heroism. I will not say of
this Company, " Esto perpetua ;" but " seu plu-
" rimas tribuit Jupiter Hyemes, sive hanc ulti-
" mam," a heavy responsibility will rest with
those who subvert it without clear and satisfactory grounds for presuming that a more perfect
system of administration will be substituted in its
place ; that the well-poised constitution of this
country will not be affected by the change ; and
that the people of India, albeit possessing no re-
presentatives in the British Parliament, will in
their future rulers find protectors and friends, acquainted with their situation and wants, indulgent
to their feelings and prejudices, determined to
maintain their rights and interests, and solicitous
to promote their prosperity and happiness.

APPENDIX

APPENDIX.

—

APPENDIX A.

STATEMENT of the Territorial Debt of India, *bearing Interest*, for a period of Thirty Years; or from the 30th April 1793 to the 30th April 1822, with the Annual Interest thereon.

	Principal. Sicca Rupees.	Interest. Sicca Rupees.
On the 30th April 1793......	5,33,68,683	45,58,798
Ditto............1794......	4,77,69,240	35,69,555
Ditto............1795......	4,77,60,064	38,66,964
Ditto............1796......	5,03,25,644	33,85,686
Ditto............1797......	5,71,29,008	35,79,716
Ditto............1798......	7,57,04,769	48,96,510
Ditto............1799......	8,49,74,559	62,73,496
Ditto............1800......	10,11,24,828	76,66,946
Ditto............1801......	12,39,42,360	90,93,323
Ditto............1802......	13,63,51,420	1,19,02,293
Ditto............1803......	14,45,73,061	1,18,81,854
Ditto............1804......	16,18,54,265	1,24,55,045
Ditto............1805......	19,09,71,445	1,39,98,771
Ditto............1806......	21,72,71,252	1,67,26,998
Ditto............1807......	23,15,30,125	1,97,13,929
Ditto............1808......	24,48,92,828	1,95,21,929
Ditto............1809......	24,33,30,220	1,96,45,058
Ditto............1810......	23,82,36,344	1,89,04,303
Ditto............1811......	21,41,19,640	1,93,06,167
Ditto............1812......	22,11,82,349	1,26,12,248
Ditto............1813......	22,68,48,000	1,37,80,000

	Principal. Sicca Rupees.	Interest. Sicca Rupees.
On the 30th April 1814...	*21,39,92,502	1,27,93,896
Ditto............1815...	†23,86,30,000	1,43,25,000
Ditto............1816......24,20,00,000		1,45,24,000
Ditto............1817......24,84,60,000		1,49,13,000
Ditto............1818......25,36,00,000		1,52,63,000
Ditto............1819......26,78,00,000		1,60,91,600
Ditto............1820... ‡29,14,10,000		1,48,50,000
Ditto............1821......27,92,31,000		1,70,68,261
Ditto............1822... §27,27,86,000		1,65,45,000

The results of the first twenty years, or from 1793 to 1812, are taken from statements prepared by the Accountant-General of Bengal in March 1813, and submitted to the Court of Directors, through the Supreme Government, in a despatch bearing date the 27th of that month. The results of the first twenty years of my account of the surplus and deficit of India for thirty years, are also taken from statements prepared by the same officer; and as these documents were formed with the utmost care and attention, I have followed them in preference even to the English accounts, which are, no doubt, of high authority.

The amount of the debt, *bearing interest,* cannot always be taken as decisive evidence of our financial situation; because we have also a debt, *not bearing*

* I find it elsewhere stated at Sicca Rupees 21,16,90,520; and the statement printed for parliament shews it to be £26,959,454.

† This sum includes the loan from the Vizier, Rupees 1,03,82,093.

‡ This includes also the sum received from the estate of the Bhow Begum, Sicca Rupees 55,98,436.

§ The debt of 1822 appears, from the printed statement, to have been £31,623,779.

interest, and because the proportion which the *assets* bear to the debt varies very considerably at different periods. Still the debt, bearing interest, is what should be kept always in sight, since it determines the annual charge, and it ought not to increase if there be a surplus of assets which can be applied to its liquidation.

APPENDIX B.

STATEMENT of the Territorial and Commercial Debt and Assets of the East-India Company, Abroad and at Home :

Territorial.—1814 and 1815.

Debt in India, bearing interest, on the 30th
April 1814 . ... £26,802,045
Do. not bearing interest do. 3,923,948

Total, Debt in India £30,725,993
Debt in England due from Territory, on the
30th April 1815......................... 5,001,531

Total, Territorial Debt £35,727,524
Deduct :—Territorial Assets 17,300,619

Territorial Deficit......... £18,426,905

Commercial.

Assets, abroad and at home, at
the two periods respectively £22,787,034
Debt do. do.............. 2,484,270

Commercial Surplus...... £20,302,764

Carried forward.........£20,302,764

Brought forward.........£20,302,764

Deduct, Home Bond Debt, principal and interest, on the 30th April 1815 (it not having been determined whether it constituted, wholly, or in part, a Territorial or Commercial Debt)............... 4,487,170

Net Commercial Surplus............... 15,815,594

Net Deficit £2,611,311

Exclusive of the Capital Stock stated at £7,780,000

N.B. In the Territorial Assets above, the sum of £400,000 is included, in part of the "Dead Stock," amounting to £12,210,896.

And in the Commercial Assets, the sum of £1,143,000 is included as the value of the India-House, and other Commercial "Dead Stock."

Statement of Territorial Debt and Assets in India.

Territorial.—1815.

Debt in India, bearing interest on the 30th April 1815................................. £27,831,877

Do. not bearing interest do............... 4,689,695

Total, Debt in India............ £32,521,572

Deduct, Assets in India on the 30th April 1815 16,401,357

Territorial Deficit in India, in 1815... £16,120,215

exclusive of Territorial Debt in England.

Territorial.

Territorial.—1816.

Debt in India, bearing interest 30th April
1816.................................... .... £28,067,964
Do. not bearing interest do............... 5,071,734

Total, Debt in India............... £33,139,698
Deduct, Assets in India 30th April 1816 16,941,813

Deficit in India in 1816............ £16,197,885

Territorial.—1817.

Debt in India, bearing interest 30th April
1817...................................... £28,821,457
Do. not bearing interest do............... 4,866,540

Total, Debt in India............... £33,687,997
Deduct, Assets 17,834,755

Deficit in 1817............ £15,853,242

Territorial.—1818.

Debt, bearing interest 30th April 1818...... £29,417,578
Do. not bearing interest do............... 5,241,703

Total, Debt......... £34,659,281
Deduct, Assets............... 17,491,987

Deficit in 1818......... £17,167,294

Territorial.—1819.

Debt, bearing interest 30th April 1819....... £31,065,547
Do. not bearing interest do............... 6,286,723

Total, Debt......... £37,352,270
Deduct, Assets 18,492,312

Deficit in 1819......... £18,859,958

2 H   *Territorial.*

Territorial.—1820.

Debt, bearing interest, 30th April 1820... £33,801,961
Do. not bearing interest do.............. 6,909,374

Total, Debt......... 40,711,335
Deduct, Assets.............. 19,506,302

Deficit in 1820......... £21,205,033

Territorial.—1821.

Debt, bearing interest, 30th April 1821 ... £33,427,106
Do. not bearing interest do.............. 7,436,344

Total, Debt......... £40,863,450
Deduct, Assets.............. 22,429,312

Deficit in 1821......... £18,434,138

Territorial.—1822.

Debt in India, bearing interest, 30th April
1822..................................... £31,623,779
Do. not bearing interest do.............. 6,967,878

Total, Debt......... £38,591,657
Deduct, Assets.............. 22,204,704

Deficit in 1822......... £16,386,953

STATEMENT of Indian Debt and Assets in 1823, and
Home Debt and Assets in 1824, taken from MS. Accounts.

Territorial.—1823 and 1824.

Debt in India, bearing interest, 30th April
1823..................................... £29,283,345

Carried forward......... £29,283,345

Brought forward......... £29,283,345
Add Bills returned to be reinvested in Loan 245,653
Debt not bearing interest 30th April 1823 9,796,339

Total Debt in India, ditto £39,325,337
Territorial Debt in England, 30th April 1824, *7,033,971

Total, Territorial Debt, Abroad and at Home, £46,359,308
Deduct, Assets in India £27,911,946
Ditto, at Home...... 1,760,669 29,672,615

Territorial Deficit £16,686,693

Commercial.

Assets, Abroad, 30th April 1823 £1,938,541
Ditto at Home, ditto ... 1824 22,746,469

Total assets... £24,685,010
Deduct, Commercial
Debt in India, 1823 £537,487
Ditto, at Home, 1824 3,335,369
———— 3,872,856

Commercial Surplus...£20,812,154
Deduct, Bond Debt in England,
April 1824 3,937,654

Net Commercial Surplus............ £16,874,500

Net Surplus upon the two Accounts......... £187,807

Net Surplus upon the two Accounts in 1823-24 £187,807
Deficit upon these Accounts in 1814-15 2,611,311

Improvement in the general result
since 1814-15 .... £2,799,118

* Of this sum £6,090,076 is owing by the Territory to the Commerce.

N.B.—The Capital Stock is not included in
the above, being...................... £7,780,000

I have only given the Commercial Account at the
commencement of the term, 1814-15, and at its close,
1823-24, as I could not trace it with great exactness
throughout the whole period, and the chief object was
to shew the result of the comparison between the two
periods.

In explanation of the great variation in the amount of
the Territorial Debt in the course of a single year (between 1820 and 1821, for instance), it is necessary to explain, that the statement only includes the debt *in India*,
and that nearly corresponding variations may have taken
place in the Account of Territorial Debts and Assets in
England.

I had prepared a statement of the Indian and Home
Debts and Assets in April 1823, in order to obviate
the objection which may be urged, that no certain
conclusion can be drawn from accounts which are
brought down to two different periods; but I found
that I could not adjust the Debits and Credits between the Territory and Commerce in a manner quite
satisfactory to myself, or which would perhaps have
been satisfactory to the reader, and I have accordingly omitted the Statement, and adhered to the Printed
Accounts, which are closed for India and England at
two different periods. The circumstance of the Company
having to render two distinct accounts (Commercial and
Territorial), and of the Indian Accounts being always a
year in arrear, renders it difficult to blend and adjust the
two, in a way to render the general results perfectly
clear and intelligible.

The above account sufficiently proves, I think, that since the commencement of the present charter an improvement has taken place in the situation of the Company, *Territorial* and *Commercial*, abroad and at home, to the amount of near three millions sterling, notwithstanding our having been engaged intermediately in several expensive wars.

I have prepared the figured statements given in this publication with the utmost care, and I have referred to the best authorities within my reach for the purpose of discovering and correcting errors, but I shall still probably have occasion to claim indulgence for mistakes, into which I may have fallen in the course of reducing into a more compact form such numerous details.

In the body of the work, where I give the general results of the accounts, I have stated the Commercial Assets in 1823-24, at only £14,424,500, whereas the Net Commercial Surplus is stated above at £16,874,500. The difference arises from my having deducted from the latter sum, £2,450,000, stated to have been advanced in India, from the Territory to the Commerce in 1823-24. If however we add the sum of £4,754,902, advanced to the Territory from the Commercial Profits, the Commercial Surplus will appear to be £19,179,402, on the 30th of April last.

APPENDIX C.,

BY H. T. COLEBROOKE, ESQ.

As very incorrect notions appear to have been entertained concerning the nature of the " *Panchágeti*," prevailing from ancient times in India, it is expedient to consult the writings of the Hindus themselves, who in treating of the administration of justice, have occasion to advert to the subject. The following is a brief summary from very ample disquisitions, contained in Treatises of Hindu Law.

An assembly for the administration of justice is of various sorts : either stationary, being held in the town or village ; or moveable, being held in field or forest ; or it is a tribunal, superintended by the chief judge appointed by the sovereign, and entrusted with the Royal Seal, to empower him to summon parties; or, it is a Court held before the Sovereign in person. The two first of these, are constituted at the request of parties, who solicit cognizance and determination of their differences; they are not established by operation of law, or by the act of the King, but by voluntary consent. The two last are Courts of Judicature, established by the Sovereign's authority : such a Court is resorted to for relief, as occasions occur ; and not as the first mentioned, constituted merely for the particular purpose.

To accommodate or determine a dispute between contending parties; the heads of the family, or the chiefs of the Society, or the inhabitants of the town or village, select a referee approved by both parties.

Among persons who roam the forest, an assembly for terminating litigation, is to be held in the wilderness;

among those who belong to an army, in the camp; and among merchants and artisans, in their societies.

Places of resort for redress, are, 1st. The Court of the Sovereign, who is assisted by learned Bràhmans, as Assessors. It is ambulatory, being held where the King abides or sojourns.

2nd. The tribunal of the Chief Judge (" *Prád vivàca,*" or " *Dharmàdhyacsha* ") appointed by the Sovereign, and sitting with three or more assessors. This is a stationary Court, being held at an appointed place.

3rd. Inferior Judges, appointed by the Sovereign's authority, for local jurisdictions. From their decisions, an appeal lies to the Court of the Chief Judge, and thence to the Rájá, or King, in person.

The gradations in arbitration, are also three.

1st. Assemblies of townsmen, or meetings of persons belonging to various tribes, and following different professions, but inhabiting the same place.

2nd. Companies of traders or artisans : conventions of persons belonging to different tribes, but subsisting by the practice of the same profession.

3rd. Meetings of kinsmen, or assemblages of relations, connected by consanguinity.

The technical terms in the Hindu, for these three gradations of assemblies are, 1st, *Puga ;* 2nd, *Sréni ;* 3rd, *Cula.*

Their decisions or awards are subject to revision : an unsatisfactory determination of the " *Cula* " or family, is revised by the " *Sréni* " or company, as less liable to suspicion of partiality, than the kindred ; and an unsatisfactory decision of fellow-artisans, is revised by the " *Puga,*" or assembly of cohabitants, who are still less to be suspected of partiality. From the award of the

" *Puga*, " or assembly, an appeal lies, according to institutes of Hindu Law, to the tribunal of the " *PrádvivÁca*," or Judge ; and, finally, to the Court of the *Rájá*, or Sovereign Prince.

The " *Puga*," " *Sréní*," and " *Cula*," are different degrees of " *Pancháyeti ;*" which, as is apparent, is not in the nature either of a jury, or of a rustic tribunal; but merely a system of arbitration, subordinate to regularly constituted tribunals, or Courts of Justice.

It was not the design of the Bengal regulations to abrogate the " *Pancháyeti*," or to discourage arbitration.

The judicial regulations of 1772, provided that, " in all cases of disputed accounts, &c., it shall be recommended to the parties, to submit the decision of their cause to arbitration ; the award of which shall become a decree of the court. Every encouragement is to be afforded to persons of character and credit, to become arbitrators; but no coercive means to be employed for that purpose.

This provision, in nearly the same words, of which the above is an extract, occurs in the regulations passed in 1780.

It is repeated in the regulations of 1781, with this addition, that " the judge do recommend, and as far as he can, without compulsion, prevail upon the parties to submit to the arbitration of one person, to be mutually agreed upon by the parties;" and, with this further provision, that no award of any arbitrator or arbitrators, be set aside, except on full proof, made by oath, of two credible witnesses, that the arbitrators had been guilty of gross corruption, or partiality in the cause in which they had made their award.

Here

Here we find the first deviation from the spirit of
Hindu arbitration : the regulations of 1781 were drawn
up by Sir E: Impey, and that deviation, which was intended to render arbitration more effectual, has, in its
consequences, overset the system. Every dissatisfied
party, unable to impeach the award of an arbitrator
without proving partiality or corruption, set about ca-
lumniating the arbitrator ; and imputed corruption to
him simply, that he might obtain a revision of the award,
which, in the Hindu system, he might have obtained in
regular course of appeal, without any such imputation.
As the practice grew, all respectable persons declined
references, lest they should be calumniated by the discon-
tented litigant; and "*Panchâyeti* " has fallen into disuse.

APPENDIX D.

PROVINCE OF CANARA.

In the " Revenue Selections," page 532, a Minute,
dated in 1816, of Lord William Bentinck, then Governor of Fort St. George, is inserted; in which his
Lordship observes, that, "from the first transfer of Ca-
" nara to the British authority, it has continued a
" solitary example of tranquillity, of an easy and regular
" realization of the revenue, and of general prosperity.
" The causes of such effects are, in my opinion, (observes
" his Lordship) to be found in the tenure of landed
" property, peculiar to the province, and in the mode-
" ration with which the rights of the Sircar, to a propor-
" tion of the land revenue, have been exercised," &c.
His Lordship, of course, confined the remark to the
districts under his own Government; because, in Bengal,
we had abundant instances of the same description.

The Court of Directors also observe, in noticing this Minute, that the " *Ryotwar* " or Field Assessment, secured to them what they conceived could be secured under no other system of management ; *viz*, the eventual advantage of an adequate revenue from the waste lands of the country ; a source which, in their opinion, under a judicious and enlightened administration of their territorial interest, it was not unreasonable to expect from past experience, would yield a considerable and annually-increasing augmentation to the public resources, &c. &c.

Now; let us see how far this expectation has been realized. The province of Canara has been under " *Ryotwar* " management throughout the whole period of our possession of it : Lord W. Bentinck notices it as the only instance of successful management ; and yet, with all the anticipated benefit from the waste lands, what is the present state of the revenue ?

Mr. Hodgson has favoured me with the following Statement of the Land Revenue, collected from Canara, during eighteen years: *viz.*

From July 1799 .... Star Pags. 437,923
Do..... 1800-1 451,409
Do..... 1801-2 448,466
Do..... 1802-3 464,930
Do..... 1803-4 463,698
Do..... 1804-5 465,093
Do..... 1805-6 466,512
Do..... 1806-7 459,102
Do..... 1807-8 465,170
Do..... 1808-9 462,994
Do..... 1809-10 458,718
Do..... 1810-11 457,911
Do..... 1811-12 458,600

From July 1812-13 ...... Star Pags. 458,987
Do..... 1813-14 458,061
Do..... 1814-15 458,836
Do..... 1815-16 455,814
Do..... 1816-17 457,042

What are we to infer from this statement? Undoubtedly, that the " *Ryotwar* " mode of management contains
no principle of improvement; that, when undertaken
under every circumstance of advantage, it remains nearly
stationary; that under it, the landholder and the peasant
must remain poor, while the Government can never
become rich. If its notorious failure to produce an
increase of revenue were its only demerit, I should never,
probably, have meddled with it; but it is a system, in my
opinion, calculated to produce poverty and wretchedness,
wherever it exists.

We have the assurance of Lord W. Bentinck, that the
Assessment of Canara was light in 1806; the Court of
Directors evidently looked to an increase of resource
from the cultivation of the waste lands; but what, after
all, has been the result? The province did not, in
1816-17, yield a larger revenue than in 1805-6; and we
have the following declaration from the Board of Revenue
at Fort St. George in 1818, that even this stationary
revenue, is more than the province can pay:

60. " To the practice of loading the lowly assessed or
" industrious Ryot, with the tax of his less fortunate or
" more improvident neighbour (condemned by the very
" officer who adopted it as both "impolitic and unjust");
" to the assumption of a maximum standard of assess-
" ment (the Beriz), much beyond the capability of the
" country, even at the period of its greatest prosperity,
" to the gradual approximation made to this high stand-

" ard, in the actual demand on more than half the landed
" property in Canara; and to the annual variation and
" consequent uncertainty in the amount of the assessment
" on individual Ryots, as much as to any temporary re-
" duced value of produce, or the imposition of new
" indirect taxes, are to be ascribed the decline in agri-
" gulture, the poverty among the Ryots, the increased
" private sale of landed property by the landlords, the
" difficulty of realizing the collections, and the ne-
" cessity, before unknown, of disposing of defaulters'
" lands, in satisfaction of revenue demands; which,
" after fourteen years residence in Canara, at length
" constrained the late Collector to record his conviction,
" that the present assessment is beyond the resources of
" the province."!!!—See Minute of the Board of Revenue at Madras, dated the 5th January 1818.—" Revenue Selections," page 898.

THE END.

LONDON:
PRINTED BY COX AND BAYLIS, GREAT QUEEN STREET

For EU product safety concerns, contact us at Calle de José Abascal, 56–1°,
28003 Madrid, Spain or eugpsr@cambridge.org.

www.ingramcontent.com/pod-product-compliance
Ingram Content Group UK Ltd.
Pitfield, Milton Keynes, MK11 3LW, UK
UKHW010340140625
459647UK00010B/732